TIME FOR A CHANGE

David Buchanan

TIME FOR A CHANGE
Copyright © 2019 by David Buchanan

Library of Congress Control Number: 2019914914
ISBN-13:   Paperback: 978-1-64398-971-6

Printed in the United States of America

LitFire LLC
1-800-511-9787
www.litfirepublishing.com
order@litfirepublishing.com

CONTENTS

CHAPTER 1

After sitting in Santa Rita jail for two years for a murder, it felt good to be finally free. As I kissed the pavement that people coming to visit were walking on, I could care less about how they were looking at me while I thanked the Lord for giving me another shot of freedom. Seeing my best friend not so fortunate ending up getting 40 years to life on the same case, you would have thought it had opened my eyes up. Yet all I knew was the hood and that was where I was on my way back to, straight from the gates.

For the last two years my young bloods had been holding the spot down and this would be a major surprise for them to see me free when everyone had already counted me out. However, things wouldn't be the same going back without Money. Once the jury said, "Guilty" to him our lives both changed.

Only 16 months had passed since I had gotten released for the murder. The newspapers were already reading, "A man acquitted in a 2001 killing was in critical condition

Friday after being shot more than a dozen times while standing in front of a shrine for a recent slaying victim, police said. Investigators said the victim, David Buchanan, 26 was found about 5:07 am in the 2000 block of 23rd ave after residents called police to report gunfire. He was in front of a makeshift shrine for Kevin Gilkey, who died Tuesday from a shooting in another part of Oakland. It was not known if Buchanan knew Gilkey, but both had ties to the 23rd ave area.

Officer Bradley Miller, who is investigating the case with Sgt. Arotzarena said Officers found Buchanan conscious and laying on the sidewalk, having just dialed 9-1-1 with his cell phone. But he was uncooperative with officers trying to find out who had shot him, Miller said.

When Officers arrived at the site, Buchanan was the only one they found. But Miller thinks there may have been other witnesses to the shooting who left before Officers arrived. Police confirmed Buchanan has a prior conviction for sales of Narcotics and has served a prison term. He was also one of two men charged in a 2001 slaying where he was acquitted, and the other man receiving 40 years to life in the State Prison".

Waking up with tubes running all over my body, I couldn't believe I let this happen to myself. I had been shot 12 times and was laying in Highland Hospital in critical condition. Everything was coming back to me and I could remember how everything had happened. Paralyzed from the waist down from a bullet lodged in my back. As my memory came back to me I didn't want to believe the people I called friends had left me there to die. I knew exactly who shot me, yet my frustration was more towards the guys who ran off and didn't even try to get me no help. Most of them

I had known most of my life. I'm sure they all thought I was dead, how he stood over me and fed me 12 bullets and didn't stop until the gun had no more bullets to shoot.

I really thought I wasn't going to make it when I laid on the pavement for 15 minutes losing blood and the first person that approached me didn't want to help me because he was scared of what might happen to him if he got involved. Laying there alone I felt like I was running out of options when it came to me to call on my Heavenly Father.

As I called out to Him in the form of praying, suddenly a bright light shined down on me from the sky and He spoke directly to me for the first time. "I was wondering how long it would take for you to call on me, my son. You're going to live. I want you to tell anyone with ears the goodness of your God. Make sure from this day forward you take care of your kids, family and most of all stand firm on the word of the Lord."

After He was done saying what He said, I was able to remain calm and collected. Before I knew it another man came walking up the street. "I knew I had heard gun shots", he said nervously. "Sir can you please help me?" I pleaded with him with tears in my eyes. Before he could walk off like the last guy did I told him, "Can you just do this for me, my car is parked across the street, it's a phone inside on the charger. Can you just grab it and bring it to me?"

Doing just as I asked, the man brought me the cell phone and I was able to dial 9-1-1 and help was on the way. I had never been so happy to see the red and blue lights coming my way in my life. Nevertheless the next set of events would be unbelievable for those of little faith.

CHAPTER 2

Highland Hospital was said to have the best trauma center in the Northern part of California. If I hadn't heard the words from my Heavenly Father myself, I would have thought that it was the trauma center that saved me as well. With nothing but sad family members around my bedside, I made hand motions to allow them to know I could hear them and was regaining my strength.

For weeks Sky would stay by my bedside, night and day. In nine days they let me out of the intensive care unit and place me in Room 346 on the 3rd floor. I was now able to have visitors between the hours of 6am to 8pm. Sky told the Doctors over me that we were married and was allowed to be the only one to spend the nights there with me. She made arrangements with my Mom to keep our son, which she agreed to with no question.

The hardest part was on Mama trying to keep the news away from my 5 year old son. I didn't want him seeing me like this. Little did I know this would be my condition for a while if not forever. The bad news came when Dr. Wyon told us I was name a paraplegic. Paralyzed from my waist down from the bullet lodged in my back. I was not sure I wanted to live life in a wheelchair.

Just as the doctor was exiting my room from delivering his bad news, the investigators were coming in.

"Hi, my name is Investigator Miller and this is my partner Sgt. Arotzarena. We will be investigating your case." The tall white guy wearing a suit and tie, with salt and pepper hair said as soon as he came in my room.

"Well good, so why are you here, the person who shot me damn sure ain't here." I told him, already mad at the world about the bad news I had just received about my health.

The fat Sgt. Named Arotzarena, who you could see hair was falling out on the top part of his head spoke up. "We're sure he's not, but we was hoping you could point us in the right direction to stop this monster before his next victim won't be as lucky as you." He said sternly.

"Sorry Sir, but if you came up here to try and get me to do your job, you came to the wrong room." I told them, knowing they both were hoping they could get a statement out of me.

Letting my attitude get the best of him, Investigator Arotzarena finally got down to business using his ace in the hole. "Well, Mr. Buchanan, so that you are aware of your situation. The ER's cut your clothes off of you, they found a bundle of rocks in between your ass cheeks, which is a violation of your parole. So when you're done here, you and your new wheelchair will be coming with us." He replied confidently.

That would be the least of my worries. After a 66 day stay at Highland, I was released to the care of the rehabilitation program to help me learn to survive as a paraplegic. This would be a six month program that would be well needed.

Eden Medical Center was located in San Leandro, California that assisted patients in achieving the highest level of rehabilitation possible. Their services were committed to restoring function to patients with problems ranging from simple mobility issues to complex cognitive concerns.

The moment I entered Eden Medical Center I was overwhelmed with how many people were in the same situation. There were wheelchairs everywhere. I felt like we were going to be playing bumper cars soon. Not letting any of it bring me down, I used it as my motivation telling myself I will be the one to walk again. Being an inpatient client in the program gave me the Physical therapy I had to have if I was even going to have a chance.

As the weeks turned into months, things started to really take a big toll on Sky, who had been my biggest physical support. She was there for me every moment she had.

The more I prayed, the more I saw that the Doctors just might be wrong about my recovery. The God I knew, could do all things and wasn't just a giving God but also a forgiving one. I made a full recovery in 9 months and was back walking. Too ashamed to let anyone other than Sky see me attempt to walk, after how many times I fell down trying.

With Officer Miller and his partner still coming up to the center checking on the status of me and a few others, on my heels still about some so called drugs they found on me. I wasn't going to wait on my discharge from Eden Medical Center. I had to go before they got wind of my full recovery. Having Sky made it that much easier to go when it was time to make my move. Pulling the car to the side of the building where they would let the patients smoke, Sky loaded me in, never to return.

My immediate family had been moved out of Oakland to a little city 30 miles out called Vallejo so I decided it was time for me to as well. Timing couldn't have been any better. Sky and my only child was just entering kindergarten and the new city felt just like the right place to have him at to start school.

To make life even better, my mother and her husband had just received a settlement for $100,000. My Mom had always been there for me, even with her drug addiction but was never able to do much in the financial department. So with the cash in hand $10,000 wasn't much to ask for. If I couldn't walk before, once I got the cash in my hands, it was now like I couldn't sit still all of a sudden.

Sky and I went out and bought two cars that same day. With us having a family a van was first. It was on 22" rims and an x-box hookup to a 13" flat screen TV falling from the ceiling. It was just right for me and my son. I also got something a little smaller for myself. It was a hardtop sky blue 1972 Chevy Chevelle SS 396. The material things started making me feel a little better about myself and my situation, which was getting better with time.

I was able to apply for Social Security Income and was approved for the rest of my life. This would be life changing. Up until this point I had never had an income on paper. Selling drugs was my income all my life. Having an income now on paper opened doors for me drug money never could.

I started looking for my own place. Now with a fixed income I didn't need anyone to help me and it felt good. However, I had all the street game, but on the corporate side of things I was an air head. I was realizing that I had spent too many years of my life wasting time running the streets. I had no credit at all, nor had I ever had a job. I had accomplished nothing and my eyes were wide open now.

For the first time in my life I was thinking clear. Sky and I had gotten our first apartment together. Just as things seemed to be coming together for us, my past came back like a wild wind.

One day as I was riding around the streets of Vallejo in my Chevy Chevelle, scoping out the city, red and blue lights appeared in my rearview mirror. Riding, blasting my four 12s speakers to the max, I was asking for trouble. When the Officer got to my window and asked, "Are you on parole or probation?" I knew this wouldn't end well. Giving him my name wasn't the right thing at all. The look on his face when he was coming back told me everything before he even spoke.

"Mr. Buchanan, we have a warrant popping up for you out of the County of Alameda. So I'm sorry I'm going to have to ask you to step out of the car and keep your hands high where I can see them" he said very calmly.

Once he learned of my situation of being paralyzed, he let me call Sky so she could come get my car and other belongings. Before I knew it, I was in Solano County Jail in Fairfield, Ca. Just as Officer Miller had promised, I was being charged with the so-called drugs that was found on me when I was shot. With this not being the county charging me, I had to play the waiting game for Alameda County to come get me and take me back to Oakland to face a judge. Being also on parole I would be seeing the parole Board before getting out as well.

Two days over a week in Solano County Jail and my name was called to get on the transportation bus headed to my next destination, which I was hoping would be Santa Rita County jail to face the new pending charges.

CHAPTER 3

Silence surrounded the bus as the transporting officers filled the bus with inmates heading to prison. Being in a wheelchair, they loaded me last. As the bus pulled away from the Solano County Jail, I couldn't believe I was once again in this predicament. I was prepared for this to be a long trip.

The bus made a hard left turn getting onto Highway 12 heading to Tracey. Placing my finger against my temple as I started to think back to the night I got shot and put in this wheelchair....

The sky was darkening into a deep blue, all of the stores were now closed for business, yet the ave was packed with people. Everyone was hanging out, passing bottles, listening to the music blasting out of Fast Eddy's 745i BMW.

"We are going to make this a night to remember", by the Atlantic Star was playing in dedication to his dear friend, Big Gil.

Big Gil was a hood OG who had put in his share of work for the hood and had just fallen victim, shot and killed in the streets of Oakland. Bringing the murder count to 89 and it was only August 18th. So the hood had come out to say their good-byes. Paying their respects as there was a candle light memorial set with empty bottles of Hennessy and Remy Martin lined up, as well as balloons, teddy bears and graffiti all over the walls. He would be forever missed, but never forgotten.

"Rest in Heaven big fella" I shouted as I rolled dice and hit another seven. The dice game had been going on for hours and had made it up to hundred a fade, It had to be my night because for the last 30 minutes I had hit every point I caught and was up over ten thousand dollars and going. Gambling had always been my thang and with the alcohol in my system I was really feeling myself. Up already a lot of money I was ready to go but I played by the code of the streets. Never quit when others were losing, so I stayed giving them a chance to win their money back, but they only kept losing more.

It was 4:23 am and down to only about seven dice shooters left when a guy with a slim build and acne skin walked up trying to get in the game. Problem was he only had sixty dollars. Handing it to me, I let him know we were shooting hundreds. His whole demeanor changed, but someone gave him the forty he needed to join the game. Before handing me the extra forty dollars, he looked me in the eyes and ask, "You Little Dave, you don't remember me?"

Looking at him I knew I didn't know him, however, him asking that made me look at him harder. But one roll and seven came and he was done with money.

Walking away from the dice game with his head down, it hit me who he was, another broke nigga, I thought to myself. Still on my knees shooting dice I never saw him reappear behind me, but I felt someone walking up. Looking up in just the nick of time to see him with a gun in his hands pointing right at me. No time at all to reach for my own gun, I just covered my head, which he was aiming for. Instead of telling me to break myself and robbing me, he just started shooting. Shot after shot went into some part of my body as I rolled on my back, kicking and screaming. Each bullet went into my body so fast I never felt any of them. Out of 12 shots, every bullet came in me and right out, except for three. One in my lower back, one in my chest and my right leg.

As if shooting me with his pistol wasn't enough, he relieved me of my pistol and emptied that clip on me as well. Then before running and disappearing into the dark, he went into my pockets and took as much of the winnings as he could......

The bus came to a hard stop bringing me back to reality. We were at Devel Vocational Institution also known as D.V.I. Prison and Reception Center. Here we would all undergo the CDCR reception center process. Where you remain on processing status until a classification staff representative reviews your case and endorses you for transfer to a mainline institution. With this process taking up to 60 days or more, this would be home for a little while, lock down most days 24 hours a day.

Me being a Parole Violator, I only needed to see the parole Board. Which was an in house hearing where they made the decision on how much time I would be receiving for my violation of Parole.

Exiting the bus we were all taken into R&R receiving where each inmate was stripped naked including body cavity search, then given a roll of orange prison clothes.

Next we were all finger printed, picture taken and entered into the system.

We were assigned to a housing unit and sent on our way. G-wing was the unit I was sent to since I was ADA "American Disability Act." I was placed in a four man cell, which catered to most of the needs of being in a wheelchair. Fortunately for me, my three cellys were all from the Bay Area. Once in the cell I introduced myself and they all did the same. It was two OG's both in their late 50's and the third dude more my age in his 20's.

He was the youngest in the cell and his name was Marvin. He was out of Berkeley, standing at an even 6 feet tall, with long dreadlocks and a muscular built frame. 295 pounds and anger issues out of this world, we had a lot on our hands with him.

The oldest OG in the cell name was Mad Dog. He was an old playa out of Richmond, but had moved to Sacramento where for him the grass was a lot greener. Now just an old washed up pimp, he had lots of game and knowledge.

The other OG was named Malone. He was originally from New York, but after spending his last 30 years in Oakland, he was a town vet.

For weeks we all got along for the most part. Until one day Mad Dog and Marvin had words that lead to a very bad ending. OG Mad Dog and Marvin had been going back and forth about how Marvin had gotten his second strike on the case he was in on now. Because let OG tell it, that was the only way he was serving 80 percent of his time.

"Youngsta, I'm in here for a possession of a firearm just like you, and it only carries, 16, 2, 3. They gave me the 2 years and with it being my second strike it doubled up to four years. You telling us they gave you 32 months, tells me they gave you the 16 and with that doubled up that gives you 32, giving you your second strike as well" OG Mad Dog stated resting his case.

"Listen here old man, it don't cost you a dime to get out of mine. I don't know what they did to you but I only got one strike so don't put me in your boat that's about to sink" Marvin said with uncertainty in his eyes, still not wanting to believe his ears. Only 24 years young and already two strikes. Yet what OG was saying sounded about right, Marvin would never admit to this one.

"Whatever you say youngsta, you will be lucky if you live to be my age, but when that counselor come and see you, just come and apologize", OG Mad Dog said as he picked up his book and went back to reading it.

The next week a moment of truth was near as the C.O. came to our cell and said, "Marvin your counselor is here to see you."

Fifteen minutes later the cell door reopens and Marvin re-entered. His facial expression said it all. We all knew he had gotten some bad news and Mad Dog couldn't wait to hear that he was right.

Cautiously, we waited to hear him break the news, but he never did. Breaking the silence, OG Mad Dog ask the question of the hour.

"So what did he say?" With the results in his hands, he look down and in a slow motion he spoke low, "they sending me to fire camp and I do got two strikes now, but I ain't apologizing for shit", Marvin stated firmly.

We all knew fire camp was miles away and everyone wanted to stay as close to home as possible, and fire camp was the furthest. And if that wasn't bad enough, he just admitted he also had two strikes, one more and he would be living life here forever.

Wasting no time, OG Mad Dog dug in like the dog he was. "I told you, didn't want to listen to old dog. I only talk about shit I know", Mad Dog said loudly with a smirk on his face.   This was the last thing Marvin wanted to hear.

"Bitch ass old head, you act like you happy to hear some shit like this, you hating ass bitch." Marvin fired off at the OG calling him more than one bitch, it was a fight in the making.

"You left your bitch at home, but I got your bitch right here youngsta", Mad Dog responded, jumping of his bunk putting on his boots.

With a look of major concern I could only hope that Malone stopped it before it was too late. Mad Dog had the heart of a giant, but was only the size of a yorkie to the guy he was up against. Showing that he didn't care at all about them two strikes he had, losing control, Marvin sprung into action, relieving all his stress and anger on the OG. Power punch after power punch, Marvin hit him landing each blow either to his face or head leaving the OG defenseless with blood running from his nose. Down for the count, the OG was done, laid over on the floor, without even getting a punch or kick off.

As night fell over the prison, our cell was still in a state of shock. No one had said more than a few words since the fight. Once Mad Dog cleaned his self up, he sat at the edge of his bunk deep in thought. He didn't eat his chow, nor did he speak a word to anyone. By the time everyone had laid down for bed I looked up and saw that OG Mad Dog was still deep in his thoughts. I fell asleep thinking he will get over it.

Element of surprise, I was awakened by the loud screams of Marvin. OG Mad Dog was standing over Marvin, driving an ink pen in and out of his body. Yet there was already one ink pen stuck in Marvin's right eye ball. Before we knew it, our cell had turned into a crime scene. Blood was everywhere as C.O.'s ran from every unit to come see the damage that Mad Dog had done. Marvin lay there motionless, awaiting the ambulance to air lift him off prison grounds and take him to the nearest Hospital in Tracey, California.

After a few days had passed Malone and I got word that Marvin lost his right eye and was back in prison in the infirmary unit. As for Mad Dog he had turned his four year stay into a life time commitment, picking up his third strike, without even getting out. Shaking my head I could only learn from this. Just the trials and tribulations of day to day life in prison.

CHAPTER 4

Before long my name was called to go see the Parole Board. I was pushed into a small room where I sat alone for a few minutes, nervously hoping not to get much time when a well-dressed, older white man entered the room. He wore a bald head, his gray beard showed his maturity.

As he took his seat, he opened my file that was awaiting on the table before him.

"Hello there, are you David Buchanan, C.D.C. Number V22474" He finally spoke and asked.

"Yes Sir, I am." I replied sitting straight up in my wheelchair.

"Well I see here you were shot over a dozen times. You are one luck guy to be standing, I mean, sitting here before me." He corrected himself and kept right on talking. "There must be a God out there and He sure must love you, young man. So did they catch the person who did this to you?" He asked more out of curiosity than any real concern.

"Not that I know of Sir", I admitted hoping he would get to the real reason we were here.

"Well I don't see you as a danger to yourself or anyone else in the position you're in. So I'm going to credit you for time served and continue you on Parole. Good luck and understand you have a purpose." He said sounding genuinely concerned as he got up and left the room.

Full of excitement to hear I was to be free, I couldn't wait to be let out of those gates. Little did I know, I was only halfway to freedom. With the hold I still had from Alameda County meant I still had to see a judge. Officer Miller had fucked me real good with this one.

Upset I would be spending a few more days still in Prison after being released, however there was still one more way out. Now that my Parole hold had been lifted, I could make bail and see the judge from the streets.

Back in the unit, I asked to use the phone and knew the right person to call. My sister Jessica picked up on the first ring. I told her I could get out tonight if she paid my bail. Before the call was over, her and her husband was on their way too Bad Boys Bail Bonds to bail this bad boy out. I never saw the inside of Santa Rita Jail. Jessica posted my bail and waited on me at the gates of the prison.

On the long ride back home Jessica had a mouthful of news to tell her big brother, who she had once again came to his aide. Yet her news was bittersweet.

While I was in prison, Sky had gotten my van towed and Jessica had to pay to get it back. Since then Sky and my son hadn't been home much. This wasn't at all what I wanted to hear. With Sky not knowing I was free, I was a step ahead of her and able to find out where and who she had been with.

We arrived at my house a little pass 9pm and to our surprise Sky and my son was home. My son was overjoyed to see his dad come wheeling myself into the house. Standing there motionless was Sky. She was only back to grab her and my son some clean clothes to wear and back off into the streets.

Looking into her eyes was like looking at her soul, and when she wasn't able to look me in my eyes I knew something was terribly wrong. But instead of being on that, I spent the night enjoying being home with my family.

The following morning I wake up to the smell of homemade French toast, scrambled eggs and fried bacon along with a glass of orange juice. The taste of freedom had kicked in as my son and I lay in bed sharing food and watching cartoons.

Sky fed us a great breakfast and headed to the restroom to take a shower. I knew this would be my best time to pick my son's brain outside of the presence of her. Yet the news he would deliver I could have never been ready for.

"Daddy was missing you when I was gone." I told him during a commercial break.

"I miss you too Dad, every night you wasn't coming home" he replied with the cutest smile.

"Son, when Daddy wasn't home, where you and mama was staying at?" I asked my son, knowing that at only five years old, the truth was all he knew and just what I was about to get.

"We always stay at my Mom's Auntie house Daddy" He truthfully said.

"Was your cousin Jason there?" I ask, which was more like a trick question, due to the fact I knew Jason was away in college now.

"No Daddy, he wasn't there, he in school far away my Auntie told me" he said repeating only what he heard. I knew he was on point now, so I went in on the bigger question.

"So where did yall sleep at?" I went on to ask.

"In Jason's room, just me, Mama and Donte." He answered blowing me away.

Donte was in the bed with yall?" I ask nervously, not really wanting to hear the answer. I knew Donte, was her Auntie's baby daddy's brother.

"Yes Daddy, every night he would sleep behind Mama and I sleep in front of Mama" he told me without even having to think about it.

When she came back into the room to join us, she was puzzled by my change of attitude. Her motherly instincts kick in and she knew her son had told me something, but had no idea what.

Playing it cool, I never revealed to her what he said. To love a woman the way I did her was dangerous but to not love her, would be torture to myself. She had been on my team for many years and she had become the strength I needed that was helping me get back to being me.

Everything that the doctors said I wouldn't do again was showing to not be true. Mind over matter, and day by passing day I got a little of me back.

The day came for me to make my first court appearance since being bailed out. Municipal Court of Alameda was held in downtown Oakland next to the Oakland Police Station. Sky and I parked and headed up to the third floor. Preparing myself for the worse, I was surprised God wasn't finished with his blessings for me. We went into department 304 and a public defender handling my case called my name. Stepping outside of the courtroom he told me that all charges had been dropped and I was free to go.

CHAPTER 5

As the sun rose above the clouds, you could feel it was going to be a good Sunday. We all were dressed in our Sunday's best to go give thanks to the Lord. With me having so much to thank him for I couldn't wait to get there.

Union Baptist Church was a church my grandmother had been attending for years. Her relationship with Reverend Pastor Mccoy and the first lady Mrs. Mccoy was outstanding and Granny loved their church. The church parking lot was filled to capacity.

Entering the church's doors, the Spirit was felt through the choir having the house rocking as they sang the words.

"I rejoice when I think about, what he's done for me." The choir sang all together. It hit me hard as I felt the Holy Ghost. Jumping for joy, praising the Lord something had come over me. Tears ran down my face, while I said a silent prayer to myself thanking God once again for all his blessings.

The choir finished the song and then Pastor Mccoy took his position at the pulpit. He asked that everyone turn their Bibles to Job, Chapter one, verses 6-21. As he read everything seemed vividly clear to me, that God puts his strongest soldiers through his biggest wars. Pastor Mccoy delivered a strong message and I left church that day knowing I had to change the way I had been living.

Traditionally, after church service it was common for us all as a family to head over to Granny's house for a nice Sunday dinner. Granny-Boo was my mother's mother. A very spiritual woman and God-fearing. She had two daughters and one son. With my mother being her oldest, they did a lot of talking. Granny-Boo's government name was Monalise, but all her friends called her Lise. She had many friends behind doing God's work. This Sunday she had put together another outstanding meal. Many other families would look at what Granny had cooked as Thanksgiving but for us it was just another Sunday dinner by Granny-Boo. She had prepared baby-back ribs, cooked so well the meat was falling off the bones, sweet corn, collard greens, honey coated cornbread, baked potatoes with sour cream, butter and cheese. And last she had mac and cheese, ham and yams.

After a powerful prayer was led by Granny-Boo, we were able to eat, as much as our bodies could handle. We all ate and were able to take plates home. Mama and I were the last to leave, due to Mama staying back to help Granny clean and wash up the dishes. When all was done we took seats on the sofa and talked for a minute.

"David, I'm grateful that you made it out to worship today. You have to remember to keep your faith, you've got to believe God when he says he will pour out his blessings that you won't have room to receive". She said all this with sincerity in her eyes.

"Giving and helping is your measure of love for Christ by obedience in your actions. David, just step out on faith, in the name of Jesus, and he'll do the rest. You see what he has done for you already and he ain't done watch what I tell you." Granny-Boo insisted.

I let her know I understood and thanked her for such a delicious dinner and sharing the wisdom she had with me. Sky and I both kissed her before making our way out the door.

With our son sound asleep, Sky and I shared a few glasses of wine and recapped on such a wonderful day. Sky drunk cup after cup. By her fourth cup, I could tell she was feeling herself as the wine started to do the talking. Kissing her around her neck making her squirm, sent fireworks to every nerve in her body, releasing all the tension she had built up holding on to her own dark secret.

She was now able to relax as we went to bed. She still knew deep in her heart after today change was coming, just not the one neither of us really wanted but would be getting.

CHAPTER 6

In the subdued light, I sat still, awaiting Sky to come out with her results of her pregnancy test. For days she had been feeling very sick and doing a lot of throwing up. So today we had decided to go to the doctor's office for her a check-up. I knew she couldn't be pregnant, because even though we had made love a few times, I was yet to have an ejaculation.

She came out and as always I observed her eyes. Lowering her head and looking everywhere but at me told me she had bad news.

"So what happen babe?" I asked as she got in the car and closed the door. No words to say she just handed me the paper in her hands.

~Positive~ was all I read before I said anything.

"Babe you looking sad, but it says you're pregnant." I said sarcastically knowing we had a real problem on our hands.

My entire incarceration she had been dealing with Donte and knew in her heart it was his. Moments later she finally answered me saying, "I'm not sad, I just don't think we are ready for another child right now."

The rest of the ride home neither of us said another word.

Once home, anxiety was killing me as we approached our room door. It was time I let her in on some of the things I knew and had been holding on to. Noticing that she was never going to tell me her secrets, I cut to the chase and asked her about Donte.

Surprisingly she came clean, only adding insult to injury. Telling me everything that my son did, yet in better detail. The foundation of our relationship was quickly crumbling. The truth is generally seen, and rarely heard, and I had heard enough to make my decision. Our relationship was over. My pride wouldn't let me reconsider. I was never the one to turn the other cheek and if I was to do so today it would be the one that the whole world could kiss.

The next morning Sky was up packing her things heading back to Oakland. Since my son was in school in Vallejo we agreed for him to stay with me. The first few weeks things went pretty smooth just father and son. Each passing day made me appreciate Sky for all the things she used to do, not just for me but also for the sake and presentation of our family. It was over now and where I wanted to be started to take its toll and within days I was riding around the streets of Vallejo looking for what the city had for me.

Mare Island Elementary School was the school my son would be attending for first grade. With Sky gone it was my responsibility to make sure I was around to pick him up when school let out at 1:30pm. Which didn't give me much time to myself at all.

Vallejo was a real nice city to raise kids in as well as have a family. A major upgrade from Oakland where gunshots and sirens were the most common sounds in the city. Riding around in Vallejo I noticed that there was next to no drug spots. What they did have was a hoe stroll. Sonoma Blvd. was a long strip where at any given day you could ride by and see anywhere from 10 to 20 young ladies trying to sell themselves.

One afternoon as I came to a red light on Florida and Sonoma, there she was looking all in my car. She was amazing from head to toe. Beautiful face, slim waist, nice size breasts, long legs and a small but nice ass that made it impossible for most tricks to ignore. Dressed in a thin, all pink, Donna Karen sundress that tied around her neck, revealing her also pink lace bra and thong set. She held an essence about herself, a certain uniqueness that was very attractive. She waved at me and wasting no time, I made a right turn at the light and pulled over. Looking in my rearview I could see her heading my way.

"Hey there handsome, you looking to have some fun?" She asked once she made it to my passenger side window.

"I sure am." I replied with a smile showing off all my gold teeth.

"Well for this here tight pussy you gone need $300.00." She said very seductively.

Looking at her like she had shit on her face I couldn't believe she got at me like a JoŠ.

"Sweetheart, three hundred bitch I'm trying to rent the pussy, not own it." I told her, hoping she got my point.

"Who the fuck you calling a bitch, you cheap bastard." She yelled out, walking away from the car, waving down the next car she felt may be a real JoŠ's.

Driving off, I had a feeling I would be seeing her again. Next time she wouldn't be getting away so easy. Continuing on my way, I checked the time and saw it was time to pick up my son from school. Smiling to myself I was starting to like the city already.

CHAPTER 7

I
t was a beautiful day out and I had finally decided to let the guy who owned the Smoke Shop on Tennessee Street talk me into selling him my Chevy for $6500. As we sat in the Smoke Shop signing over the pink slip and counting the money, a customer came in to get a pack of backwoods. Hearing it, I knew it was a female voice, so I came from out of the back office to get a better look.

She had brown skin, smooth and healthy looking, with a rounded nose. Her cheeks set up neat, transient hollow dimples when she smiled. She wore the usual, jeans, neatly starched and faded. A navy blue button down that was a few sizes too big, but tucked in neatly above her slender hips and rounded ass.

Everything about her I liked, and nothing about her was hood. Making my move I stepped from behind the counter and helped her by being a gentleman and opening the door.

"Why, thank you." She said politely.

"You're more than welcome, with your beautiful self." I replied.

31

"Again, thank you for the compliment, but with them big sunglasses on how can you say you can see anything clearly?" She jokingly asked.

Removing my sunglasses I was wearing off of my face I responded.

"You're so right, you're even more beautiful without them." We both laughed as I reached my hand out and introduced myself to her. Doing the same thing she shook my hand and said her name was Sherise. Over a few laughs I was able to give her my number more so on her trying to buy weed, but it was a start.

That same night as my son and I were in the house playing Xbox 360, I get a call from Sherise. She was looking for some weed and I had some for her. I had sold my car and just bought a pound of some purple indo weed. Giving her my address it didn't take long for her to pull up.

Taking her the weed outside, I was taken back on how pretty she really was. We sat outside my apartments getting to know each other better. Her level of conversation alone was like no other woman I ever had. She was very intelligent and a hard working single parent. After a hard break up from her first love and only child's father, she was in no rush to trust another man. Hearing that I too had a son and just like her I was living as a single parent, she only wanted to learn more once she heard that. Outside so long, my son came outside looking for me. Seeing the little handsome fellow herself melted her heart and she fell in love with him on the spot. A love for children and a motherly instinct, she knew just how to win him over as well. We said our goodnights and promised to call her and make sure she made it home safe.

That first night we must had stayed on the phone until the sun came up. Something I hadn't done with a woman since grade school. From that day we were either on the phone with each other or she and her son was at my house, or my son and I at her house.

It was time for Spring Break and Sky had my son and I had the weekend alone with Sherise. Her son was also gone for a few days. Unfortunately for me, it had been over a month and a half and all I had gotten was a kiss out of her. I was growing more and more attracted to her and felt this would be my weekend with both kids gone.

Sherise's demeanor set her apart from other women, yet I was wearing her down and no matter how hard she tried to resist me, she started to break. She wasn't trying to fall in love, but after six months of being alone, tonight she felt herself giving in as our tongues explored each other's mouths. Palming her ass as we shared a passionate kiss, setting us both on fire. One thing lead to another as she held my hand and led me to her bedroom. Following right behind her the door opened and she slowly came out of her jeans. Standing there in only a bra and thong that rounded her ass was devouring, I loved what stood before me.

Clit throbbing and dripping wet, she finally walked close enough for me to touch her and I took control. Laying her down on her stomach, I eased into her from behind. In and out, slowly as I picked up speed making the headboard of her bed hit the wall, harder with each stroke. With both hands sshe pushed the headboard to stop it from hitting the wall so hard, while arching her back in the air so that I had a perfect shot, rubbing on her clit. Sending a pulsing sensation through her body, helping her reach an orgasm, immediately, as tingles ran up and down her spine. Feeling her orgasm on my rock hard penis felt so good, made me have one myself. As I came, she came again. Still shuddering from the after effects of multiple orgasms, I held onto her and fell asleep.

CHAPTER 8

'm just a bachelor looking for a partner, someone who knows how to ride- were the words I wake up to, as "Pony" by Genuine was playing on BET on her TV. Looking at her naked body reminded me of what an amazing night we had. Not wanting to awake her, I showered before leaving, kissed her on the cheek and made my way home.

She lived in the downtown part of the city in the projects called the Vistas. Being in the Vistas made me feel back at home. The apartments were dominated by Black families and to me a great place for drug sales. I could tell the guys in them were selling out of them, but nothing like it would be if I had my hands in on the action.

Pulling out of the project gates in my Chevy Van on 24" inch rims, the looks on all the young playas faces said a lot as they all did their best trying to identify me, as one put up a thumb in acknowledgement of how clean the van was. Hitting the horn back at him was my way of saying Thanks as I made my way out, thinking in the back of my mind, "One day these apartments will be mine."

By noon my phone was ringing and I was surprised to see it was Sky. I didn't have to pick up my son from her for another few days, so I was hoping everything was okay as I answered.

"Hello." I picked up.

"Big David this me," she said like I didn't know it was her.

"I know who this is, what's up beautiful?" I asked feeling good and trying to get to the reason for her call.

"I'm sure you tell everyone they're beautiful, but however I want to know have you been having a bitch around my son?" She boldly asked.

"What in the world are you talking about, your son?" I asked needing to know when did he become just hers.

"Nigga don't act like you don't know what I'm saying. My son told me some girl name Sherise, who has a son, been spending the night at your house and some nights yall go to her house and.."

Cutting her off, I interrupted her. "Listen here we not together, so don't worry about who I have at my house." I let her know but she wasn't done.

"Well it's my right to know who you got around my son. I'm uncomfortable with that so I think it's best if he just stay out here with me and go to school out here." She announced like she had it already planned out.

This was a moment of truth and the biggest decision I would have to make. Since she had been gone, having my son alone hadn't been easy at all. The responsibility was heavy, but one I could do and had signed up for. Yet I was missing being able to come and go as I pleased. After a few moments I made the worse decision of my life. Giving up without a fight, court date, nothing just saying, "If that's how you feel, then go ahead keep him with you. I'll just get him on weekends." I said, hating myself for every word.

Hanging up the phone, I had to call my mom, the one person who was going to tell me what I should do. In two rings she picked up.

"Hey son, how are you doing?" She answered with lots of joy in her voice.

"I'm doing okay, just wanted to talk to you about a issue I got." I told her with uncertainty in my voice.

"Is everything okay David?" She asked starting to get very concerned.

"Yes everything fine, I just need some advice." I told her.

"Well when you come over here, I'm cooking and all your sisters and brothers are here, we can talk"

I agreed and headed to her house. Mama's home cooking and some family loving was just what I needed to feel better.

At the door my nose was greeted with the smell of fried chicken, macaroni and cheese, mashed potatoes, baked beans and dinner rolls. Like always Mama was in the kitchen doing her thang. Standing around the kitchen doing more talking than helping was my three sisters, Jessica, Sarah and Asia. I gave them all hugs as I grabbed a piece of chicken and took a bite.

"Boy, you ain't washed your hands, nor is all the food done." Mama barked at me like she always did. Leaving the ladies in the kitchen, I continued through the house to the back yard, where I knew I could find my brothers. Joshua had a backwood in his hands smoking, while Dwayne our youngest was rolling another one up. Passing the wood to me, in the same motion as giving me a hug, Joshua asks, "Where my nephew at?" Asking about the whereabouts of my son. Feeling like it was my best time to tell them since he asked, I told them about the agreement I had just made with Sky.

"No way, big bruh, you didn't agree to that." Dwayne said sadly.

"I know I shouldn't have went out like that, he all I got." I stated, before taking a hard hit of the backwood. Flipping the script I asked how things had been going with them.

At the dinner table I told everyone about Sky and my decision. They all went in on me for not being the man I was meant to be and fought for my son. Jessica, Mama's second child, was the most upset with me. Making it her business she called Sky herself.

Sarah and Asia both assured me that they had my back. This was just the kind of love and support I needed. When dinner came to an end, we all headed to our own homes as full as could be.

CHAPTER 9

Living for today, preparing for tomorrow was just what I was doing. With my son no longer at the house I was out seeking big rewards, which meant taking bigger risks. I knew the streets played for keeps and one minor slip could lead to a major fall. Thoughts of where I was and where I wanted to be, filled my brain. In life a man chooses his own journey, where he ends up is purely a reflection of the decisions he made along the way. So my next decision was either about to make or break me. I had to go back to what I knew best.

As I saw the welcome to Oakland sign, I knew it was show time. Riding with a glock nineteen on my lap I just wanted to score and get the hell back to Vallejo. Seeing the 23rd exit, I got off the freeway headed to the hood.

Foothill ave, cross 28th street and when I reached that destination I was glad to see my young bloods, Sterling, Chris da 5th, Thurm, Greg and Ant P's all still holding it down. It felt good to see them, but being back on the block brought me back to an unbelievable state of mind. I still couldn't believe the verdict of guilty they had come back with for Money. Thinking to myself how I had told him and did my best to get him to take the deal they were offering us. Seeing it end in the worst possible way made coming back very depressing.

I got my package and said my good-byes and got back on the highway heading to Vallejo. Sterling had made sure I got everything I had needed. Looking into the bag I knew I was back at it like a crack addict. Ten ounces of powder cocaine, for $4500, was winning, when in Vallejo they were starting at $800 a ounce.

Making it home I said a silent prayer, thanking God for the safe trip back home. It was time to get in the kitchen and make magic happen. I had the dope with no one to sell it to. One thing I did know was that good dope sold itself so once Vallejo got some of this I would.

CHAPTER 10

The atmosphere couldn't have been more perfect. Sherise and I sat at her kitchen table with two glasses of red wine and a chess board between us. This was very intriguing to me. She was the only female I knew who not only knew how to play but was damn good. My interest in her escalated as we vibed very well together. Loving the facts about her having a good head on her shoulders and more impressive was her independency, working a nine to five doing Medical Billing for private doctors. With her level of confidence and strong will I knew it wasn't anything we couldn't accomplish together.

Finding a woman with confidence to be very sexy, I couldn't stop from lusting over her smooth skin, long pretty wavy hair and light brown eyes.

Calling checkmate, I knew I had underestimated her. With it being her first win out of ten, I smiled with plans of checkmating her tonight in a different game.

After chess, I decided to take her out of town for dinner at one of my favorite joints in San Francisco called Thang

Long. Wearing an all red long sleeve, Ralph Lauren jumpsuit, which had open front slit from neck to waist, showing off her voluptuous body, she was ready to go.

As we rode the Highway 80 crossing the Bay Bridge, I could see she was enjoying the beautiful view of all the lights over the water. San Francisco was a wonderful city and as she used her phone to take pictures to capture the moment, I smiled just seeing her happy. Enjoying every moment until we pulled up to the restaurant's valet parking. We had front door service and as sexy as she was, she deserved it.

Holding the door for her so she could enter first, with her plump ass that shifted its weight from side to side every step she took. Definitely demanding attention as soon as she entered the room.

In minutes we were seated and both ordered a drink as we awaited our waitress. She ordered more red wine as I got a shot of Remy XO. When the waitress arrived I ordered the shrimp fried rice and whole crab and she got the Barb-q-sautéed shrimp, charbroiled catfish with another glass of wine.

On the long ride home, she fell asleep half way across the Bay Bridge. Being with her felt good and had signs of me finding love again. Love was still the ultimate adventure.

CHAPTER 11

The sun was shining bright which was typical for California weather. Up and out early, trying to be the first to get the worm, since I had sold next to none of the drugs I had. Being under Sherise, I wasn't doing much more than enjoying every moment she had to give. However after getting a call from a young lady I gave my number to weeks ago, today I had different plans.

Drea was her name and with her man going to jail just nights ago, leaving to her out here she was a lost bitch. Being originally from L.A. she moved to Vallejo with her boyfriend after they had ran him out of Long Beach for ratting on his connect when he was caught with a pound or two of weed and a loaded Mack 10. Already on bail for a firearm, he decided to tell on the connect to free himself. Not being able to go back to Long Beach, he had a grandmother who stayed in the Bay Area and talked his girlfriend into coming with him.

With only an aging grandmother in Vallejo, things didn't come easy for him nor his girlfriend. Doing everything they could to keep money in their pockets, he noticed his grandmother's next door neighbors were leaving on a vacation. Thinking he had found an easy lick, he waited till nightfall and did a home invasion. With the Asian couple not believing in banks, it didn't take him long to find what he had come for. Hitting the jackpot, he came up on $26,000 in cash, an Alhambra water jug filled with coins, as well as a jewelry box of gold rings, bracelets and chains. Not knowing the house was wired with video cameras that recorded visual images and sound. Lucky for Drea, he needed her outside as a lookout so she never entered the house. On camera they had him and only him on the inside of the house.

Digging a hole in his grandmother's backyard they buried most of the cash that same night. Feeling like they had gotten away with it, he had Drea going to Raley's change machine turning in all the coins for cash.

Wasn't many days before the police was at his grandmother's door raiding her house. Once they came home and saw the video, they saw him very clearly. The jewelry box was found in his grandmother's house along with him.

Drea had just missed being in the raid herself. Out getting them some food saved her. Pulling back up to the house in a cab, police were everywhere and her heart told her what for. Waiting it out, she went in when they were all done. His grandmother let her get her things and told her she was no longer welcome there. Nowhere to go, she decided to call the guy in the Chevy Van and see if he could be of any help.

Drea stood at an even 5' 7", very thick in all the right places. Straight out of the shower, she moistened her body with Victoria Secret body lotion. One look in her full length hotel mirror she could only think back to how her body 'used to be before having kids. Now with the stretch marks, flab and cellulite she just wasn't as confident as she used to be. She could only hope she could make a good first impression on me.

Motel 6 on Fairgrounds was where I had to pick her up. After talking on the phone, we had made plans to take a trip out to San Francisco to the tenderloins district to make a few dollars off the drugs I told her I already had.

The downtown part of San Francisco was called the tenderloins, where you could buy anything from a ten dollar bag of weed to a kilo of cocaine. It's the city that never sleeps and an easy place to make a few dollars or two. On our way, I got to learn a few things about Drea. One was that she wasn't telling me everything I needed to know. What I did get a clear understanding about her was that she was homeless, her boyfriend was in jail and if she didn't make something happen tonight, she wasn't going to be able to pay for her room.

We made it into the city and parked on Golden Gate street. Taking her on a tour of the area, I hit the main streets. First was Turk street, then up Ellis and ended on 6th and Market street. Every street we hit she made money on. She liked the way she was able to make sales with no effort at all. In two hours she was telling me all the drugs we came with were gone.

Taking her back to her Motel, I paid on it for two more days relaxing her in more ways than one. Inside her room she opened up to me, telling me her life story. As well as got into more detail about what really happened to her boyfriend, which was like music to my ears, hearing about $26,000 still hiding in some old lady's backyard. I had to look more into this interesting information.

At 26 years old, Drea had two kids down in Los Angeles, ages four and two, being cared for by her baby daddy's parents. Making very bad decisions, Drea was now crying for a way out. I wasn't too sure if I was the guy for the help she needed.

The next few weeks we were together every day going to the Tenderloins making more money each time. She built a relationship with me and before long I started letting her just stay at my house.

Drea and I started working together well, and the only thing that was on my mind was getting to that buried money in her boyfriend's grandmother's backyard. Every day we would ride pass the house, plotting and planning a way to get back there and make away with the funds.

Drea knew from living with the old lady that on Mondays she left the backyard gate unlocked for the garbage men to get the trash cans. So we knew it would be a Monday night. Since she had helped him bury it she had to come with me.

Four in the morning right before the sun came up, Drea and I dressed in all black hoodies and were on our way to get what she said should be $26,000 in cash. I parked a block away and walked down to the house. Shovel in my hand, I could only hope no one saw us this late and called the police. Just like she said the gate was wide open. She led the way to the area. Moving the flower pot that was covering the spot out the way, I went to work digging. Only after a few good digs and up came a leather hand bag. Dropping the shovel I grab the hand bag and open it. Heart skipping a beat as I saw nothing but hundred dollar bills. Leaving everything but the money I ran heading for the car. Her right behind me, we ran non-stop to the van without being seen by a single soul.

Excitement was what we both felt once we got home. Counting twenty six thousand dollars wasn't something I was doing everyday so I was loving Drea for this one. Throwing the money up in the air letting it rain on both of us, I already had plans on how I was going to spend it.

"I told you daddy, you thought I was lying." Drea said proudly.

It no longer mattered what I thought, she had put us twenty-six steps ahead of the game. Rubbing her hands over my bare chest, she was ready to mark her spot. Sliding down to her knees she unbuttoned my pants. No way at all was I going to stop her, as she pulled out my manhood and began sucking. The sucking got more rapid, making my dick only harder.

Moving her head in a steady motion without using her hands, was outstanding. I only could wonder, where in Christ name did she learn that one. Swirling her tongue around on the head of my penis, while I looked down into her eyes. Her soft lips taking me in until I could feel my legs getting weak. Bringing the cum out of me, I lost control. Holding the back of her head, I shoved my dick down her throat, as I released myself on her tonsils.

CHAPTER 12

The money was burning a hole in my pockets. Before Drea was up, I was out the door.

My first stop was to see Sherise. With her having great credit made her worth more by itself. Having her and her check stubs was all I needed to leave from Cal. Worthington Motor Vehicle lot with a 2004 cocaine white, Dodge Magnum with a hemi engine. We made a deal where no banks nor loans were needed, he promised us that the pink slip would be in the mail in 2-3 weeks.

Kissing Sherise out on the lot, I thanked her and let her know we were going out tonight. She agreed walking back to her car leaving me to ride off into the sun in my new Magnum.

Hearing the hemi engine told me I was about to have some fun. Heading to my next stop, I got on the freeway and headed to Oakland. My young blood told me he had me again, as we made a deal for ten thousand this time.

Fruitvale, in front of Willie Brown's Liquor store was where Sterling and Chris was conducting their business at. Pulling to the curb neither was surprised to see it was me.

"What's good with my big bruh?" Sterl said leading the way into the store.

"Same old shit, different day little bruh." I told him, handing him a bag of money and hug at the same time.

"See you got that hemi thang out there, you clean big bruh." Sterl told me as he passed the work to me he had hid under the counter.

"Thanks, little bruh, that hemi run hard." I told him leaving out the store.

Seeing Chris sitting in my driver seat made me smile as all the memories hit me at once.

"This thang sound good and inside clean too." Chris said, getting out the car.

"You got this now, you don't need the van, let me cash you out for that?" Sterl asked making his move on it. With Chris rap career now making noise in the streets, the van was something he could be in the back of as they rode the streets. His new album Master Piece showed he had more than talent, he was in question of being the best coming out of Oakland.

"Yall can come get that van anytime yall want." I told them knowing they were serious.

"Okay, we coming to get it tonight, we need that. This nigga got a show tonight we need that thang." Sterl said closing the deal for later that night.

Purring like a kitten, the hemi sounded so good as I got sideways down the street, showing off for my young bloods as I got off the gas and back to reality and what I had going on. Getting to the freeway, I headed North.

Drea had laundry done and had also got in the kitchen and put together our first homemade dinner. She made a tuna casserole, with mixed vegetables and a side salad with Italian dressing.

Wearing nothing but a thong, she was awaiting my return. Entering the door, the aroma of good food filled my nose. Seeing her in her thong set the tone for where things were going for the night. When she saw how much dope I had she knew it was time to get to the money.

She had never saw this much dope. Sitting on my lap, helping me bag up the drugs, she could feel my hard dick up against her bare cheeks. We bagged, ate the food she made and the call came in that the young bloods were outside ready to get the van.

They pulled up and the look in her eyes when she saw the 99 SS Camaro with new candy red paint and red 22 inch rims to match, said she was digging it, and so was I. Letting him keep his money, we made a deal for the Camaro for the van, straight trade. I now also had a Camaro too before the day was over.

Ready to ride only because we had a new car, Drea and I decided to head out to the tenderloins early. In the Camaro, all eyes were on us and once in the city, I had got a gut feeling that something wasn't right. Parking on Sixth Street, we walked down to Market St. to Donut World that stayed open all night.

It was starting off to be another good night as she made sale after sale. Playing look out from the corner, I kept my eyes on her. Looking so hard in her direction, I missed seeing the ATF pulling right up on me and jumping out. They had been watching us from afar and had us on a player one and two case taking us both to jail for sales.

CHAPTER 13

850 Bryant Street was the address for the County Jail and Courthouse. We were taken there and booked both on sale charges. With me being on Parole and her having a no bail warrant out of Los Angeles for Prostitution, they dropped the charges as we awaited transportation to other jails and prison in my case.

From San Francisco County Jail, I was shipped over to San Quentin to deal with my parole violation. Giving me 12 months, I was stuck and had to face the prison term ahead of me. Calling my little brother Dwayne, I knew I could count on him to handle a few things for me. Since my sister, Jessica had already gotten my SS Camaro out of San Francisco, I needed him to go to my apartment and get all the money and drugs and put it all in the trunk of the SS Camaro and park it at Jessica house. Also give the Magnum to Sherise. Next thing needed to be done was my apartment. With 12 months to do, there was no way I was going to be able to pay the rent so I agreed to let my Mama and youngest sister take over. Moms had been looking for something smaller to stay in. With all her kids out on their own she didn't need a big house anymore.

After forty-seven days in San Quentin reception, a bag was given to me to put all my belongings in. On the bag it read:

David Buchanan #V22474

Corcoran State Prison.

Corcoran was a mainline Prison, four hours south of San Quentin. I was placed and housed on Corcoran's B-yard. It was medium security, living in a dorm setting. I was grateful for that, the cell life wasn't for me.

My first day on the yard, I ran into a few cats I knew from the streets. Dre was a guy from my hood, so it was a treat for us to see each other. I had been trying to catch up with him on the streets and was unsuccessful. Word out was he wasn't selling drugs no more, they had the whole white collar game on lock. We spent every yard walking laps, as I picked up on as much of the game he had for me. The way they was eating I had to learn.

I also ran into my good friend white boy JoŠ. His skin was white but his soul was black. Him and Dre had become road dogs, and Dre knew he would eat good in his new line of work. They made plans to hook up on the streets, we all did.

The chow hall was where we ate our meals in. Given a metal tray, that was divided into four sections. Each section filled with a different food, goulash over noodles, green peas, pinto beans, with one slice of wheat bread. Taking our trays, the crew and I filled in the open seats.

"Man, I swear this the kind of meals they give us being funny. How you gone give a nigga green peas and pinto beans, this shit don't even go together." Dre complained about the food.

"Man, in just a few more months we will all be eating lobsters and steak, counting money, far away from this place." I said, meaning every word, as I had to laugh at how white boy wasn't listening to nothing we were saying as he mixed the two beans together and went in.

Other than hanging with them two fools, I also spent a lot of my time writing, visiting, or on the phone with Sherise. She was truly someone special to me. I could really trust her. This was something new to me, because half the time I didn't trust myself.

We had love and a friendship, the sanctity and celebration of our relationship that not only supported a good life, but was creating one. Each visit we shared, we left each other closer than before. Her telling me she had been approved for a loan on her first house, she would be moving out of the Vistas Projects. She asked me to move in and make her home mine. Agreeing, I made plans to be coming home to her. Tired of running in the opposite direction of the love of my life.

"Son, she is a very mature young lady and she's going to be someone you can grow with and help you become an even better man." Mama said to me, showing she really liked Sherise. Before we got off the phone, Mama also told me that some young lady and a guy came to her door looking for me. Sharp as a tack, Mama told them she just had moved in and never heard of the person.

Giving me the description of both of them, I had a gut feeling who the young lady was, but was lost on the guy.

With me only ever bringing three women over, Mama knew two of them, leaving one unaccounted for. If it was her with a dude, told me one thing.

CHAPTER 14

I t was never about where you started, but where you ended at. Ending my joke at Corcoran and ending up with Sherise was exciting. For a guy who was once a paraplegic, I got out in great shape.

In her black fitted dress that accentuated her hour glass figure, showing more cleavage than needed to be she was captivating. Rushing over to where she was parked, standing outside of the Magnum, I picked her up off the ground while we kissed. Palming her ass, I never wanted our kiss to end.

Jumping in the driver's seat, I pulled out of the parking lot heading back north. Looking at the prison in my rearview, I knew I would never be seeing that place again.

Making it back to Vallejo felt the best. Mama had the grill out and a bar-b-q, party was well on its way. My brothers and sisters all was there, as we enjoyed food, music, drinks, table games, and most of all each other. Loving the freedom, air and all the family support, it was no way I'll be giving this up, ever again. I had to come home and do something different. However, with a trunk full of drugs and money it was going to be hard doing that. Getting everything out of the trunk and getting it in the house brought me back to reality to where I was at before going to jail and where I was headed.

Overwhelmed by the house Sherise had made ours while I was gone. Loving what she had accomplished, I walked around the three bedrooms, two and a half bath, up and down stairs. Two car garage, backyard with a hoop court, I felt like a tourist in my new home. Making my way upstairs, I was hit with the hot, steamy, shower Sherise had just exited grabbing her towel. Relieving her of her towel, I dried her back off, as I playfully popped her on her rounded ass. Kissing on the back of her neck, as I stepped out of my own pants. Turning her around so that she was facing me, I began to suck on her luscious nipples only turning her on more. Laying her down on her back, I kissed down to the parting of her legs. Slipping my tongue between her inner thighs, intensifying the moment.

Pulling her pussy lips apart revealing her pretty pink pearl. Sucking around her clitoris, then on it. Circling her hips she smothered her juices over my face.

"Oooh shit", she moaned loudly.

Grabbing the back of my head, she glided me in the motion best fitting her. Letting the heat from my mouth drive her crazy, her eyelids closed in ecstasy.

Inching down slowly, I stuck the head of my penis in her. Pressing her lips against mine, our tongues wrestled as she wrecked on my stiff pole. Fighting to make it last as long as I could, but by the time she hit what had to be her second orgasm, I gave in to the urge to fill her tight little pussy with my hot creamy nut. Hitting my peak, she cried out for me not to stop, as she came again. Her cunt pulsed around my dick, coaxing one more tiny blast of liquid from my balls.

Like T-Pain, I was sprung and so was she. After a perfect night we became inseparable. The next four years I stayed only with her, discharging my parole. She even helped me get my wholesale license, allowing me to sale cars. I even got a new job as a merchandiser for Coca Cola. Life couldn't have been going any better and before we knew it Sherise was pregnant with our first child together.

CHAPTER 15

He was 7 pounds and was born on the same day I was shot 12 times only three years earlier. He was a true blessing for me. Naming him Damonte', I looked into his eyes and vowed to be the best dad ever. Making many bad decisions with my first son David, mostly always unconcerned. None of it I could get back. This was my second chance to do it right for both my sons.

My obligation was now to my three sons. Sherise came into the relationship with a son and he was now mine too. Getting Little David a lot more, made sure my kids knew each other. With them having such a big age difference, Little David, seemed to bond better with my step-son, who was more his age. Mar-Mar was his name. Only a year and a half younger than Little David and they had a lot in common, one being the same brother.

As each weekend passed, me and Little David grew a better bond. By the time the summer came, Sky and I had agreed for him to spend the summer with me. I signed my boys up for their first sports team, softball. Vallejo Giants was our team and with there being practice on Tuesdays and Thursdays, followed by games every Saturday, I had my hands full.

The more they understood the concept of the game, the better they got. Not taking neither of them long to figure out their strong suit, Little David was a power hitter while Mar-Mar had the speed. Each Saturday they would do something to make me proud of them. When the season was down to its last Saturday game our whole family came out to support the boys. If they won they had playoff hopes. It was another gorgeous day in California. A great day for a baseball game. With family and friends cheering, my boys were ready. Little David played short stop while Mar-Mar covered left field.

First inning went easy as the first two kids up to bat hit ground balls to Little David, which he stopped with making the easy out at first. By the top of the eighth, the score was three to five with our Giants down two. Little David had been up four times, striking out three times and a pop fly also for an out. Mar-Mar had batted four times as well. Stroking out two times, and the other two he hit grounders right past the first basemen getting himself on base. The game got good when a teammate hit the ball knocking Mar-Mar in for a score, giving the Giants their third point.

At their two minute water break, I could see much frustration on the boys. Taking the water break as a time to talk to them, I had a few father to sons words. Pulling Little David to the side, I told him, "Son you're doing great out there. Just relax and keep your eyes on the ball." Nodding his head, he let me know he was following me.

"Boys, yall know what a giant means?" I asked as Mar-Mar walked up.

"It's not the name of the team, it's what you both really are. A legendary human like being of great size, strength and power. Now go out there and show them what a Giant is." I said, hitting them both on the top of their helmets pushing them back onto the field.

Time was running out and with two outs and the smallest kid on the Giants up to bat. We all thought it was over. Surprisingly, he got a base hit, bringing us all to our feet. As his own mother jumped out of hers, proud of her son's hit. The game wasn't over and next up was Little David.

"Take your time son!" I yelled out to him, as we all were still on our feet.

He stepped up to the plate and my heart was racing like a schoolboy with a crush on his second grade teacher.

The pitch was on its way, a little high, but Little David swung away, making a loud connection with the high pitch. Like it was in slow motion, we all watched as the ball went deep and over the gate for my son's first homerun of the season. Everyone went wild as the game was now tied up. The next batter had the game in his hands, if he could score the game would be over and our Giants off to the playoffs. He wasn't that luck as he struck out, sending us into extra innings. The Giants were rejuvenated after Little David's homerun, with a new faith that they could do it.

Desperations set in on the other team and they had two batters come up and both got good hits. The first got a double and the next hit him home ending the game, also the Giants season.

I was still proud of my boys and of myself. It was the best summer ever. When summer came to an end and Little David had to go back to his mother, he nor did I want him to go.

CHAPTER 16

School was back in and my youngest son was now able to do daycare with my mom, giving me plenty of time to get into something.

Candy paint on my SS Camaro was still looking good three summers later, as I pulled into the Homies Store across the street from the Vista Projects Apartments, drawing all the attention on me. The August heat had everyone and their mamas out sitting on their porch enjoying the weather.

On my way into the store I ran into an old school friend of mine from childhood. Mookie was his name and getting money was his game. He was from 34th and Chestnut in West Oakland. We attended elementary school together and he was a fool then and I was sure he still was.

At least an hour we stood infront of the Homies Store, talking, catching up on old times. Mookie let me know that he had a spot in the Vistas, and was doing his thang along with his female. Telling me, us together could run circles around this city and end up rich. I knew he wasn't lying but I knew the risk.

As we were talking three females came over to the store, Mookie hugged all three of them. The last one asked,

"Mookie, who is this fine piece of chocolate you over here talking to?"

"This my cousin." Mookie said, laughing at how wild she could be.

Eyeing me as she caught back up with her friends, hoping that I would say something to her, but I didn't.

"Dave you really need to come down here with me, it's really wide open for us." Mookie continued to tell me.

Exchanging numbers, we shook hands and went on our ways.

Every time I would be riding around, I made it my business to go pass the Vistas Projects to see if I would see Mookie. Every time no matter what time of the day it was, he was either on his patio or in front of the door.

One day as I was passing by, Mookie jumped in the middle of the streets stopping me. Moet bottle in his hand, he opened the door and got in. We hit a few corners smoking and drinking the Moet. It felt good being in the company of someone who really knew me. With all my real friends either in jail or dead we had a lot in common.

When we made it back to the Vistas, he had a few females who stayed in the back he wanted me to join him as he went to their apartment. Getting inside the apartment, I noticed it was the same three ladies from the other night at the store. The one who seemed to have an eye for me, wasted no time telling me her name was Keyona.

Keyona looked to be Puerto Rican and Black, standing four feet, nine inches with long curly hair. After a few minutes of small talk with her I knew her biggest problem. She most definitely was an alcoholic.

The dark complexion one name was Shonna. Shonna was a little heavy set, but not overly fat, with a nice ass that made her shape acceptable. She was the hustler of the three. Night or day she was ready to get to the money. The advantage she had over the other two was she was from Vallejo and knew everyone.

The third female was Mookie's girl, Kisha. Kisha was light-skinned with her hair cut into a bob hairdo. With two kids she had no drive nor hustle about herself. She was lucky to have Mookie. One thing she did like to do was fuck. Her and Mookie would head to their room to get it in even with a house full of people.

That night all we did was smoke weed, drink and listen to loud music. Mookie and Kisha headed to the room and could be hear making love. Leaving me in the living room with two drunk bitches who both wanted some dick. My attention was more on all the smokers and snorters coming to the door trying to buy drugs. I knew I would be back and from that night I was there every day.

CHAPTER 17

The game only ends in one or two ways. Death being the most common or Prison if you're lucky, I was always told. Yet I had plans on being the first to change that.

One thing about the Vistas Project Apartments was it was never a dead moment. Most of the residents were young, single mothers on welfare. Their babies' fathers were either in prison, dead or just deadbeats. In either case they were all looking for the next balling nigga to come hold it down. Not knowing, nothing came simple for a woman addicted to life on the edge. Which always came with its own set of consequences. Seeing that many of them were naïve, I was looking to take full advantage of my situation.

Never being the kind of guy to go after the women I liked, I was more into the ones who liked me. Not having to look too far as she was headed my way. Dressed in her all white Versace dress, with a long split coming up the thigh area, Keyona was looking very attractive.

Talking to her, I learned that she was willing to do just about anything to be down with me. I told her all about my relationship with Sherise and not even that changed her mind. I liked that and made plans with her that night.

Since getting out of prison, I hadn't sold any drugs but I still had a gang of it. The cash was gone, but I had a plan on how she could help me get it all back and then some. Mookie house was already the spot and with her being there already every day, I planned to start giving her drugs to sell for me.

Hearing my plan for her, she was with it and that wasn't the only thing she was with. Looking me in my eyes as we sat on the couch, she spoke.

"You know sooner or later you gone have to give me some of this chocolate." Reaching over and placing her hand on my mid-section.

"Well you know they say chocolate melts in your mouth not in your hands." I responded reluctantly, with a smile.

She could feel my manhood hardening with her hand on it. Taking my words as an invitation, she started unbuckling my belt, then pants. Finding what she was looking for, she leaned over and put as much of me inside her mouth as she could. Sucking on it like a blow pop in the summer heat. Enjoying every moment as she was putting in work. As if the head wasn't enough, once I had cum, she swallowed it all like a shot of Hennessey, taking it to the extraordinary and improbable to be believed. Leaving me quivering as I got up to leave.

On my way home she was on my mind, and I knew if her head game was that good, I couldn't wait to feel that pussy. Laughing to myself, as her new nickname came to me. Blanket lips.

CHAPTER 18

First day of fall and it had demanded that time be set back an hour, making the days longer and the nights shorter. One thing about time, was it went backwards, it goes forward, but it never stop.

The days being longer gave an early bird like me more time to hunt down my prey. Keyona was on top of her game moving anywhere from five hundred to a thousand a day, and in no time I was selling to the users and sellers. We had the best dope in the city, and controlling all the money that came to the Vistas Projects.

Change came to the Vistas once they went under new management. The new manager was a black woman named Monice Williams. She was about thirty-five years young, with a body full of obvious curves. Originally from New Orleans, she spoke with an accent that was different but sexy. Ms. Williams, what she liked to be called, was very ghetto and took the job for one reason and one reason only.

Hurricane Katrina had just hit her home city hard and this would be a way she could help her family and friends from New Orleans who had all just lost everything and needed a place to stay so they could rebuild their lives. Being the manager she could rent to whoever she pleased and that's what she did.

One by one, families pulled up in U-Hauls moving in. In less than 60 days, she had rented out 20 units, all to Hurricane Katrina survivors. They were not only survivors, they had come to survive by any means. Doing any and everything to get back what they had lost. The stories they told went from losing dogs to parents, then from homes to cars. Ending up in California with nothing more than the clothes on their backs.

The things they showed up with in U-Hauls was mostly things they had stole, took, or was given on the long ride from New Orleans to California. The hurricane was a downward spiral of grief and crimes. An internal wound many saw never healing. Leaving most of them mentally drained and physically exhausted.

Overnight the Vistas changed, and not for the better. When they would leave they left in groups of five or more. Out taking any and everything that wasn't bolted down. Turning the heat up in the Vistas. The police started coming around a lot behind them robbing, stealing and even shooting at people. Police coming seeing all the traffic we had going on at Mookie's house, wasn't long before they came over unexpectedly.

It was 6 am and the A.T.F., D.E.A. and many other law enforcements had set up a plan to raid Mookie's apartment. Mookie, Kisha, Keyona, Shonna, Joggs and one of the New Orleans cat named Pistol Pete, were all inside Mookie's apartment. Lucky for Joggs, he was up already on his way to the store when he saw unmarked cars pulling up and jumping out. Running to the back room where Mookie and Kisha was, Joggs yelled, "It's a raid, 5-0 is coming get up."

Mookie had a crawl in space in his upper part of his closet where him and Joggs hid in, before the police got in the house. The ladies did their best to flush the drugs, but with the water being turned off they had no success. Pistol Pete went for the window, but seeing nothing but armed police that way, he tried to join Mookie and Joggs, which couldn't happen. At his very last second, he buried himself under a pile of dirty laundry.

The ladies were arrested first. Then Pistol Pete was discovered under the clothing. As the police was takin Pistol Pete out the room, Mookie and Joggs heard him saying,

"It's over yall the got, just come on out." Unable to believe their ears, Mookie nor Joggs was coming out willingly. In thirty minutes of raiding, the police found three handguns, three ounces of rocked up cocaine and six of uncooked cocaine, along with sixty-six hundred in cash.

Just as the police was about to leave, the officer who had walked Pistol Pete out asked.

"So, why did you say come out yall when we found you? Was there anyone else in there?"

No one heard him say it, but when the police headed back in and came out with Mookie and Joggs, they all knew he gave them up.

CHAPTER 19

Missing the raid wasn't the only thing I had missed. I also missed the drama the New Orleans people had going on behind Pistol Pete going to jail.

Everyone was booked into the Solano County Jail, on all the same charges but Pistol Pete, who for giving up the last two, got set free hours later. Signing a statement telling everything he knew about how the house was ran.

At the arraignment Keyona and Shonna were both "OR". Mookie had a parole hold and Joggs a probation hold. Kisha on the other hand got most of the charges put on her due to her name being on the lease, giving her a bail of one hundred thousand. Mookie called me right after court asking me to get her out and he would pay me back. I put up the cash and Kisha too was freed. Once he got his discovery package he needed me to do one last thing. Catch Pistol Pete snitching ass.

Taking the necessary precautions, I went and got me a 2004 S55 Benz, with smoke grey tinted windows, preventing me from being seen. As I pulled into the Homie Store, Nate never saw me.

Nate was one of my good friends who was fresh out of prison and back to get everything he didn't the last go around. Nate was a true hustler and instead of selling hard drugs, he sold the best weed in the city. Which the Vistas didn't have but needed bad. Standing with his sidekick, Koda Mack. I got out of the car and greeted them both.

"Look who they let out the cage." I playfully said to Nate, as I stuck my hand out to him.

"My nigga Dave, the man I been looking for" Nate replied, shaking my hand.

He wanted to talk business so we got into the car and took a short ride. He needed the line on the best purple weed around, he also wanted a little hard rock for his sidekick Koda Mack.

Koda Mack was really more like his brother, they had grown up together. But Koda Mack wasn't much on the drug selling, he liked to dress nice and fresh and let a bitch pay him. I was able to line Nate up with both. Before letting him out I ran him down on the changes around the Vistas. Telling him the situation with a new guy around named Pistol Pete, who I been looking for. Getting what he needed, I dropped him back off at the store where Koda Mack was awaiting him, with a fine, short, thick young lady who started looking at the ground when I tried to make eye contact with her.

Nate took over the Vistas with his purple weed, he had no competition at all. In only two months he was buying ten pounds, not looking back. Keyona and Shonna were still getting their issue even without having Mookie's house.

CHAPTER 20

The sky was a cold grey and the wind was icy as I pulled into the parking lot of the Coconut Grove Club. Tonight Nate was having his birthday bash here and all ladies were in free until 11pm. With a special performance by Chris Da 5th, it was for sure the place would be packed.

Joggs had finally gotten out and was riding shotgun with me. Getting out of the car, we both had on Armani suits and dressed to impress. Neatly trimmed, with sideburns that wrapped around my face into a goatee, I was knocking someone's girl tonight. I could feel it, as all eyes in the long line waiting to get in was on us. Straight past the bouncers we went, and after showing our V.I.P. passes, he lifted the velvet rope and we were in. A Hostess led the way to the V.I.P. area.

The party was going great as Chris Da 5th took the stage and sang back to back hits from his album Master Piece. With everyone going crazy as we sang along word for word with him. Needing a drink, I headed to the bar where I felt someone staring at me. At the end of the bar I saw her. Smiling flirtatiously at me trying to keep my attention. Locking eyes she dipped her finger into her glass, pulled out a cherry and sucked on it, while looking me in my eyes.

Every bit of five feet seven inches, very slim, dressed in her tight little blue Gucci dress with the matching Gucci heels and handbag. No doubting she was fly. The dress emphasized her slim figure as she stood up and headed my way.

Eyeing her the whole way to me, as a smile immediately creased my well-trimmed face as she stood before me. Like a perfect gentleman, I stood up as I extended my hand, telling her my name. I was determined to meet this fascinating woman, who came to me. So that we could better hear each other, I led the way outside to my car where we talked for a minute.

As we got comfortable in my heated leather seats, she let me know her name was Punkin. She admitted she had been seeing me and waiting for this day. She let me know she was different than what I was used to. She wasn't into selling drugs like Keyona, she made her money using the world's oldest profession. Prostitution.

The moment she said that I knew where I knew her from. She was Koda Mack's bitch. When the party was over, I talked to Nate and Koda Mack about the bitch acting like she was looking for new management. Koda said he had too many to worry about one. That was my key to walking away with my first hoe bitch. But I would learn she wasn't a hoe bitch, she was a prostitute, very big difference.

Knocking Punkin proved to be a major game changer for me. For the first time I was picking up game from a woman. This was the pimping game, where you had to stay down to come up.

Even though Punkin was a true prostitute, she had a few set rules about her game, she had to make at least five hundred dollars a day. This goal she not only set but made daily. She started early in the mornings. She called it, before and after work. She would catch tricks before work, and ones who had graveyard jobs, caught them getting off. This was her best times from four am to eight am. She would usually make her goal for the day then. I liked the pussy selling better than the drugs. For one, we never had to recoup nor did we ever run out.

Keyona saw how close me and Punkin were getting and decided to start selling pussy as well. Keyona was by far prettier than Punkin. But Keyona would learn fast that Punkin was a professional at this sport and knew more than one way to skin a turkey. Her greatest asset was her mouth piece. It was the subtle things that she did or wore that could make almost any man aroused if he was allowed to come to close to her. She had game and a warm heart and was very wise.

Keyona had my best interest at heart. From day one she had my back and now with her going so far to selling herself, I knew I was on to something.

CHAPTER 21

A t home my relationship with Sherise just wasn't the same. With females now willing to do anything just to be with me, I started losing interest in love. More and more I could feel my heart turning to concrete.

Sherise was still as beautiful as she was the day I met her. Honey skinned complexion with deep dimples that enhanced her face when she smiled. A college graduate, highly intelligent, who enjoyed making an honest living. Even though I loved her dearly, I was chasing something I had never had. That was a harem, and the way Punkin and Keyona were now getting along and working together it was looking like my harem wasn't far away.

I was twenty toes down and with Punkin being my bottom bitch things were looking very promising. As we were crossing the Bay Bridge, the weed smoke filled the car as Keyona rode shotgun passing me the backwood.

"Daddy get off on Mission, that's where I want to start at," Punkin told me from the backseat.

She had been leading the way for the last few weeks as we hit a different city every night getting our money off the concrete. Tonight we were in the city on a, weekend. Keyona got out the car wearing a Roc-a-wear fitted dress that matched her skin tone, very short and revealing.

Punkin had on a burgundy tennis dress with no panties on, very short and revealing as well. Both ladies had their nails manicured, painted to their liking. Feet also neatly pedicured painted the same color of their hands.

Clubs were packed, as well as the streets. Pulling away from the curb after letting them out, I was up and down the blocks in the Mission district trying to knock me a new hoe. Parking in an alleyway, I got on feet to see what I could come up on. I wasn't doing no choosing, I was out trying to get chose. Most of the hoes wouldn't even look my way and the ones I caught working on my side of the street, would either cross over or jump in the middle of the street and walk.

As I was walking a P.Y.T. with dark black hair, that came down to the middle of her back, her skin tone was the same color as her hair, jet black. Very smooth, she was petite, but sexy with a very sassy attitude that you could read by the way she walked.

"Well what you doing working around this late?" I asked her, seeing that I had her talking.

"Shit the same thing as you, trying to get some money." She boldly admitted.

"Is that so, well let me tell you, I ain't trying, I'm getting all mine. The only thing I'm trying to get is you at this point." I told her, meaning every word.

"I heard that, you a pimp or something, because I like your style." She asked looking me in my eyes waiting for a response.

Laughing I asked her, "Matters what you call a pimp, because I don't call myself no pimp."

"You know what I mean, do you got any hoes?" She asked trying to explain.

"Well then no, because I got prostitutes." I proudly stated.

Not believing me, yet still very curious, she continued to walk with me and asking me many questions.

"So where is your Prostitutes you say you have?" She continued with her questioning.

"I hope not doing what you're doing." I replied, as we both laughed at the same time.

Trying to explain her situation, she said, "Well my dude fucked up and rather get high with my hard working money than worrying about me. So slow niggas get left." She cold heartedly said.

"I like you little mama, my name is Dave and yours?" I introduced myself.

"Nice to meet you Dave, I'm Star." She said as I grabbed her hand and kissed the back of it.

"Well damn. A pimp with gentleman ways, I heard the hell out of that." She jokingly said, making us both share another friendly moment together of laughter.

Ending up right where I had parked, I hit the unlock button on my car and saw the look on her face.

"This your car right here?" She asked with a surprised look on her face.

"Yes it is, and about to be ours if you're on the winning team." I said, giving her a shot at winning for once in her life.

"You sure your hoes ain't going to be tripping or your baby mama?" She asked starting to believe I just might have some Prostitutes.

"I already told you I don't deal with hoes and you will never meet none of my baby mamas." I replied confidently, as she got in and closed the door. I had me another one.

CHAPTER 22

Star was five feet, five inches with very long jet black hair. She was a slim goodie with a round booty. Only 23 years old, she had already been selling herself for seven years. Growing up in the city of San Francisco, Hunters Point area, nothing ever came easy for her. The only child of two dope fiend parents, she had decided at the age of sixteen to use what she had to get what she wanted.

We hit a few corners as I let her enjoy the smooth ride of my luxury S55 Benz. We reached the corner where I was to be meeting Keyona and Punkin at. I noticed Punkin getting into an all-black Bentley GT, with an old white guy driving. As the Bentley passed us, Punkin and I made eye contact. I knew by the looks of the old man, that if he wasn't hooked with any law enforcements, he was someone well worth knowing.

Pulling over so we could wait on them, Keyona pule dup getting dropped off by a Mexican guy in a work truck. The look on Keyona's face changed when she saw Star in the front seat. Handing me the four hundred and eighty dollars she had just made as she closed the door. Counting the money in front of Star, I introduced her to Keyona.

"Babe, this is Star and Star this is Keyona." I politely introduced them to each other. Pulling away I received a text message from Punkin with an address of her location. Arriving at a 20 story building in a neighborhood full of Victorian houses, mini mansions and a few brick homes. Each one gated in with very long driveways. Punkin came out with a very big smile on her face. Getting in she handed me a large bank roll and said,

"Daddy who is this beautiful young lady you have here? Hi there, I'm Punkin, I love your hair."

"Thank you, I'm Star and it's nice to meet you." Star said blushing, liking Punkin already.

I appreciated the way Punkin always welcomed other females around us. As I finished counting her tonight's take in, nineteen hundred, I appreciated her for a lot more.

Smiling, trying to hide her excitement, Punkin knew she had hit a homerun, and I wanted play by play information on how she came back with the bank roll in two hours. On the ride back to Vallejo she told us the story.

CHAPTER 23

Richard Roberts was the guy's name in the Bentley GT, but he liked to be called, Buddy. He turned out to be a millionaire who was the co-owner of ESPN Sports channel. He was 68 years old and had a penthouse on the very top floor of the building. His penthouse had no blinds over the windows, being so high up he didn't need any. Feeling on top of the world as you had the perfect view over one of the finest cities in the world, San Francisco.

Framed pictures of him and all the top sports legends hung from his wall. Buddy was not only a big time trick who loved the company of young ladies, but he also was addicted to crack.

Hating taking the risk of getting caught buying it, he like to find the girls who could also bring some with them. Today he had found just the girl. Punkin promised him she could get the drugs for him any and every time he called. Reminding him that she didn't sale drugs only pussy so when he called to make sure it's first about pussy then the drugs. Loving the sound of it he put her on his top list of call girls.

This was great news and Punkin had hit the jackpot, and with ten more toes down, so did I.

We made it back to the apartment I had recently rented for my girls. I let Punkin and Keyona out and had plans for Star for the night. Knowing she hadn't paid me yet, meant she couldn't stay at the apartment, yet a room would get us through the night.

Checking her into the Marriot Hotel, we got the last room with a hot tub inside. Stepping in it also had two beds, a flat screen TV and a small bar with kitchen. Her on one bed and me on the other, we sat back and talked as I got to know more about her, before she headed to the bathroom to take a shower.

Still dripping wet, she exited the bathroom headed to me already in the hot tub. Her dark chocolate skin was flawless, with her hair pinned up so it didn't get wet, she was wine fine. Trying without success to cover her firm breasts, she just dropped her robe as she came up the few steps leading into the hot tub. Turning on the power jet sprays, she got in and started to relax. Moving in on her in a teasing motion getting her hot all over. When she couldn't take it no more she whispered in my ear like there was someone else in the room.

"Do you have a condom?" she asked.

Looking deep into her eyes I told her, "No and I won't need one". Little did she know I wasn't here to fuck her, I came to get the money.

"Okay, I get it, you a real one." She said, stepping out of the hot tub leading me to the bed she was on, reaching in the coat pocket she pulled out one hundred and ninety dollars and handed it to me. Going down on her knees she said no more. Kissing on my penis but not sucking it, she teased before taking a mouth full. Letting me fuck her face until I was fully satisfied and my penis had went limp.

CHAPTER 24

"**G**ood morning ladies." I greeted Punkin and Keyona as I entered the apartment earlier than expected. With such a great night I had plans to have a great day with my ladies.

"Why you up so early?" Keyona asked, turning over trying to get the sun out her face.

"I have a few things I want to do with yall today. Shopping being one." I told them.

Hearing shopping, Keyona got to her feet and headed to the bathroom to freshen herself up, leaving me to talk to Punkin. Punkin not only being my bottom bitch but also my top money maker, I had something special in mind for her.

"You know that Lexus you been saying I should get?" I began to say once Keyona was out of sight. "Well I decided since you liked it so much, I should get it for you." I told her, making her happy about the new news.

"Daddy stop playing with me, you really gone let me shine like that?" She continued to ask.

"Sure am, so get dressed because that's just one of many plans I have for the day."

Full of excitement she headed to her room to get dressed. When they were both dressed and ready to go, I called Star to let her know I was on my way to get her. Part of my game was to make sure Star was with us to see how good working bitches get treated.

Kay's Autos was located on Tennessee Street in Vallejo. Kay was a very old white man who had been selling cars all his life. He did trades and in-house financing. As we pulled into his car lot, it was good to see the Lexus 400 still there. Punkin jumped out the car in her booty shorts and headed straight to it. Mr. Kay had something more than lust in his eyes as he approached her asking could he help her. Deciding to stay in the car and see how much of a deal could she get on her own, I played it from afar.

Just like a pro, she got a great deal and also found out that Mr. Kay also liked to buy pussy and Punkin let him know she had lots of it for sale. They made arrangements to meet up when he closed later that day. Keyona got in with Punkin as they pulled off the lot looking good in the Lexus on twenty-two inch rims. Impressed with my moves, Star finally had me in the car alone and shared a few of her thoughts.

"I see you take good care of your girls, I can't wait to be treated like that." Star shared with me as we followed Punkin back to the apartment where I parked my car and we got in the car with them. Riding in the back, behind the tinted windows, Star and I enjoyed the ride to our next stop. Nordstrom's.

Nordstrom's was the best store for the ladies. Everything from name brand clothes to shoes, heels, jewelry. If they looked like money just maybe they would make some. Getting everything they wanted, we headed back while the day was still young. The day had been good, but I knew the night would be even better.

CHAPTER 25

The girls all went in to get dressed for the night. It was Star's first time going inside of the apartment I had for my girls. It definitely impressed her to see how nice the inside was. Brand new everything from the living room's new red leather furniture to the sixty inch flat screen TV that had been mounted to the wall, down to the Persian rug that covered the floor. Which she wasn't sure if she could walk on with her shoes. The bathroom was just as clean with the red matching sets of towels and shower curtains.

Just like that, Star had saw enough and from that day made her mind she was a part of the family. With all their new clothes on they were ready to hit the streets and get every dime back for a real nigga.

On our way out of the city. We passed by the Vista's Projects. Surprisingly we saw Nate and Joggs standing in front. They still had the projects turned up to the max. Pulling over, I got out to have a few words with the two good men. Nate let me and Joggs know that he had found out where Pistol Pete had been hiding. This was just what

Mookie wanted and we were that much closer to getting the job done. We all made plans on hooking up on the late night.

Already having two dates lined up, Punkin was looking hot in her white and red skirt, with a button up shirt that was tied in a knot on one side, so she was ready. Mr. Kay was ready to give us some of her money back. Dropping her off on the corner of his car lot so that he didn't see me, she walked the rest as I let the other two off on Sonoma Blvd. to see what they could catch.

In the hour that Punkin was with Mr. Kay, Keyona had scored big. Landing herself in a small city nearby named Napa. Star also had gotten a date for eighty dollars. Feeling like that wasn't enough she made a few calls to her P.C.'s (Personal Clients) getting two of them to agree to seeing her for the night at two hundred a piece in San Francisco, right where Punkin had to be next to see Buddy. Having to make a decision, I took Punkin and Star to Punkin's car and cut them loose to go handle their dates, while I stayed back to go get Keyona.

Napa, California was only ten minutes away from Vallejo. Very small town known for making wine. The address she had sent me lead me to a restaurant named Los Rosa's. The restaurant was closed but I could see a few Mexicans entering using the side gate. Seconds later, Keyona came running from the side gate very happy about something. Hopping in the car she handed e seven hundred dollars and wasn't ready to go yet.

"Daddy, where's the other girls at?" She asked, in a rush to get back in there. I could tell she had been drinking, something I stressed to all the girls not to do on the job.

"They both had dates in the city so I let them go." I answered her.

"Damn, I really needed them, it's too many guys in there for just me." She complained. The owner was giving each girl one hundred dollars just to dance and entertain his guests of about fifteen drunk Mexicans. This was something he wanted to do every weekend, but didn't have the girl power. I had to meet this man and Keyona made it happen.

The back of the restaurant was still being built. It had a full bar, tables and a D.J.'s area with about fifteen people and room for another twenty, he had just the spot for a weekend hangout. There was two other girls there, one with her top off letting two guys suck on her hardened nipples. The other one was in the restroom where they were turning the tricks at. Keyona brought the owner over to meet me and went back to working on the drunk Mexicans.

"Hello, my name is Camacho, nice to meet you." He introduced himself.

"I'm Dave and it's nice to meet you as well." I told him, shaking his right hand.

After talking with him for twenty minutes, it was clear to me that he was selling ice as well as alcoholic beverages after the legal hours of sales. What he didn't have were women who could keep his customers entertained and spending money. I made sure he knew I could get him anything from ass hole to zebra booty if the price was right. We hooked that moment and from that night me and Camacho did nothing but good business together.

CHAPTER 26

Meanwhile, in the city, Punkin and Star was running it up on Buddy. Star had handled her two tricks and when she was done Buddy told Punkin she could come join them saying, "Two is better than one."

Star entered the penthouse and was told the rules. Women were to be nude in the penthouse at all times. Given $800 she was undressed in record timing. Loving the outstanding view, Star walked from window to window taking in what the whole San Francisco looked like a night.

Buddy took a full pull of the crack Punkin had brought him. Noticing the nice ass Star had on herself, he called her over to where he was.

"I would like to know could you play with your pussy until you orgasm for another two hundred dollars?" He asked her with a smile.

Thinking to herself, I could do it for a lot less, but answered him saying, "Yes Sir, indeed I can."

Buddy watched as she put on a show for him. From one finger inside herself to two. She played with her fat, juicy pussy with one hand, using the other one to caress her nipples. Slowly as she picked up speed, only playing with her clitoris, moaning out loud until her legs started shaking and fluids ran down her legs and hand like the Mississippi River. Enjoying the site he was witnessing as her eyes rolled to the back of her head.

Picking up his glass pipe, he asked her could he also blow smoke up her asshole. Turning around and putting her ass in his face, she waited as he took a "Mack blast" hit, using both of his hands he spread her cheeks apart until her asshole was open, then blew a mouth full of crack smoke in her ass. This would be the easiest thousand dollars she had made without having sex. Together the two left his house with thirty-five hundred dollars. On the way home the two ladies sang word for word, Mary J's, "Share My World", laughing together about how Buddy enjoyed blowing smoke up each of their asses. This was something they both could get used to.

Keyona and I had also made it out of Napa with over a thousand. Dropping Keyona off at the apartment, I met up with Nate and Joggs. Pistol Pete had been waiting on Nate to bring him some weed. Running down the steps and cutting across the grass, he was almost to the awaiting car when he saw my face. Never seeing it coming, it was too late for him to run back. Two shots in the back of his head as he fell to the ground, breathing heavy as his soul began to escape his body. Eyes still open, he died seeing who killed him.

Never was I the type to just move on impulse alone, but I had thought this one through, thoroughly.

CHAPTER 27

Mexicali Rose was my favorite Mexican food spot in Oakland. Not only did they have good food, but a full bar. The girls had a three hour date with Buddy so I dropped them off and went for drinks and dinner alone.

Alone eating rice and beans, with three hard tacos and a strawberry daiquiri, I watched the Warriors beat down the Los Angeles Clippers. Smiling to myself as Curry hit another three pointer to put the game out of reach.

Looking up I saw two of my good friends coming in the door. White boy and Dre .I hadn't saw neither of them since prison, but the streets was talking and I had been hearing they were on top of their game. Seeing me, they came over and joined me. We joked around, had a few shots a piece of Xo an when it was time to pay the game came out. Dre, pulling out a credit card payed for all our meals. Bringing him something back to sign, it was as easy as that.

It was the slider game. I wasn't hip to it at all. Only thing I was sliding was these bitches from city to city about my paper. But they were making fast, easy money and everything was free. Before we went our separate ways they made sure I understood what I needed to get started in the sliding game.

"I get it, an embosser, a reader writer and a laptop." I told them, making sure I knew what to do to get rich fast. I listened to everything they were telling me and once outside I was a believer. White boy jumped in a new model Jaguar and Dre got in his Aston Martin DB9. After getting the girls that night and them bringing home a little over ten thousand from one house, I knew I was going to get a new car.

Cal Worthington Motor Vehicles was the spot I had gotten my Dodge Magnum from. He knew I would be coming to get the AMG R500 Mercedes, after talking to Sherise. Giving him fourteen thousand cash, he agreed to put it in her name again and let me drive off.

The R500 was a mixture of a minivan and a car. It had three rows of seats and in the back of each seat was a TV. Heated seats from front to back, with the panoramic view. The V-8 engine made by AMG, with 390 horsepower making it easy to go from zero to sixty in seconds.

With no effort at all, I was having money. For the first time in my life I was able to buy whatever I wanted and not care about the cost. The feeling was great and my greed for more wasn't going to let me stop. I was more addicted to the lifestyle than the women bringing all the money to me.

For months the girls had been eating good off Buddy and Camacho. Things were like clockwork and we were not sure if Buddy liked the girls or the crack, but we liked the money. Camacho's weekend thang had gotten so big we needed more girls and Punkin found some. Keyth and Tiff were their names. They were like cousins and wouldn't never commit to paying me full time yet they had to pay to play at the Camacho restaurant with me which they both did. Tiff was the baddest of the two. Very tall, with pretty eyes and very big tits on a petite frame. She really had the hardest time paying me seeing four others already. She felt I didn't need hers. Little did she know I needed hers and her for a lifetime commitment. Nevertheless on our next outing, Tiff would learn just how important it truly was to have me around.

Camacho and his friends were having a Bachelor's party and was in need of at least 6 girls. I had five and felt like Ice Berg Slim, as I arrived in my R500 and all the doors opened letting out five beautiful ladies ready to get paid and laid.

The house was very big and nice, with many bedrooms upstairs and downstairs with an indoor pool area. There was Mexicans everywhere. I didn't like the atmosphere, more so how many were drunk already and seeming to be pretty aggressive. Calling all the girls over to me, I gave them my game plan.

"Okay, I can't watch all of yall, so before you go off with any of them in this big house let me know so I can keep up with you all."

Each time one of the girls would be going to attend one of the guys in another part of the house they gave me the heads up. All my main girls did as told, and after each date came and handed me over the money. Keyth wasn't my bitch, but was very much so digging how I got down and would always give me my cut.

Walking around the house, things seemed normal until I got upstairs. I could hear someone yelling over the loud music. Opening the first door, I invaded on Star on her knees giving one of the Mexicans head with her mouth full. Closing the door fast, I kept moving in the direction of the yelling. Opening the last door at the end of the hallway, I saw a Mexican holding Tiff down trying to have his way. With her fighting back he was getting nowhere fast. Rushing to her aid I knocked him off of her seeing that the only thing she had revealed were her big nice tits, I knew he hadn't raped her, yet. I still ran in his pockets and took all the money he had, two hundred and ten dollars.

"You okay baby girl?" I asked her as she was putting her tits back into her bra.

"Now I am, bitch motherfucker got mad because I wouldn't let him fuck me for seventy dollars. I was going to let him suck my tits that was about it." She explained, but still upset but grateful that I came when I did.

"This is why I told yall to let me know where yall was going." I told her as we walked back downstairs.

"My bad, I really thank you for having my back." She said, very sincerely.

That day forth she had no problem giving me my issue. But choosing up she never did nor did Keyth. However, Tiff and I learned a valuable lesson that day. In this game no one is to be trusted.

CHAPTER 28

The morning air felt good against my skin as I stepped into the morning sun. Opening the garage, I picked the S55 Mercedes for the day. Plans of having breakfast first, I stopped by the Joy of Eating and ordered me an over medium egg webbed with cheddar and draped over an iPhone thick hunk of hardwood smoked bacon smothered with chipotle ketchup and served on a fist size brioche bun. Taking my order to go, I headed down to the seven flags detail shop.

Getting out my car and handing my keys to the pretty young cashier who already knew how I liked my cars detailed. They always made sure my cars were spotless, inside and out. Rims shining extra black magic on the tires. Windows crispy clear and the inside smelling brand new.

Hitting up the gas station next, to fill up before going to get my girls, I ran into the most beautiful girl I had ever seen in Vallejo. Standing at least five-eleven, with a unique skin complexion. Red, is what I called it. Long hair, petite with long curvaceous legs that I couldn't help but notice in her summer dress. She was Super Model gorgeous with an incredible resemblance to Tyra Banks in the height and body.

"Can I help you with that?" I asked her offering to help pump her gas as I jumped out of my car.

"Are you sure that's all you trying to help me with?" She jokingly said, seeing in my demeanor that I wanted more.

Before either of us could speak another word, I found out she wasn't riding alone, as her sister came walking out of the gas station with lots of goodies.

"What's up Dave, what you doing talking to my sister?" Her sister said, as she got into the car.

"Sis, you know him already?" She asked her little sister.

"For years, that's Asia's big brother." Her little sister told her, like I wasn't standing there.

I knew her little sister from coming over to my Mom's house hanging with my youngest sister, but to me they were still babies. But this Red thang she was with today calling her sister, I wanted every bit of her in my life.

"Asia's big brother, I've never saw you around, but I hear your name is Dave, mine is Liesha." She said, seductively more comfortable now that her sister knew me.

Taking her hand into mine, her fragrance had now invaded my nostrils with delight now that I was so close to her.

"Like I was saying my name is Dave---"

Cutting me off her sister in the car said, "No it's money making Dave." Laughing, but making sure her sister knew I was getting my money, even her young ass could see that.

"Nice to meet you Money making Dave, nice car you have there as well." Liesha said, looking over at the car I had just got out of. She gave me her number as I pumped her gas before being on our ways.

After getting my own gas, I texted her phone on the spot.

"Hi, this is Dave, lock my number in, I would love to take you out and really get to know you." Pushing send and then I drove off.

That whole day Liesha was on my mind. I couldn't shake the thoughts of her unique beauty. She was a must have for me. After many hours had passed, I debated on texting her again and decided to wait it out. It seemed like forever, but at 8:28pm, I got the text I had been waiting on.

"Hello Dave, this is Liesha. I met you today at the gas station. If you're not doing nothing tonight, maybe we can catch a movie or something simple."

Wasting no time, I replied. "Hey beautiful, don't ever make me wait that long, I been thinking about you all day. LOL, I would love to, what time will you be ready?" I sent the text and just like that we had plans.

It was well after midnight by the time I finally got her back home. We saw the movie Notorious which was a biographical drama film that followed the life and murder of a well-known rapper by the name of Christopher Wallace. Once the movie was over we went out for a bite to eat at Benihana's. Giving me a kiss on the cheek, she thanked me for a good time and went in the house.

Every day after that night we were together, either at her apartment or she was riding with me to handle my business. She had a daughter that was one year old and with me having a son six months younger, we made plans on taking them out one day with us. The more time we spent together the more I fell for her.

Her knowing I had hoes didn't run her off and that was very surprising since she wasn't into the lifestyle herself.

However, she did start wanting to accompany us to see was I really pimping or talking. This would be a big mistake and rule one on the list of things never to do.

CHAPTER 29

"**D**addy, if you could take a vacation anywhere in the world, where would you like to go?" Punkin called me and asked.

Wondering why she called me asking me something like that when she was up in the penthouse with Buddy, should be getting crack smoke blew up her ass, but I answered her saying, "Miami, Florida for Memorial Day weekend."

By the time she came down from seeing Buddy, she had twenty-seven hundred dollar bills and the confirmation numbers for a round-trip for two to Miami, Florida for 6 days in a luxury place overlooking South Beach.

Memorial Day was two months away and it was a good thing it was. Punkin getting tickets for two, knew exactly what she was doing. I had time to get them on the trip or have plans for them while I was gone, because one thing for sure was I was going and so was my bottom bitch.

Liesha had a job at Walmart as a Sales Clerk and whenever she wasn't there she was riding co-pilot with me, with my girls in the back. At first it wasn't no big deal to the girls. But it seemed like the more tracks we pulled up to and they all had to get out and walk the blade leaving Liesha in the car with me, I started to feel the envy.

Day after day the girls' spirit would change once she came around. Not one of them would speak to her nor were they on top of their game. So out of their game, one night as we played the city of San Rafael. Star got picked up for solicitation of prostitution. Walking passed the bowling alley, a white man pulled up on her and Punkin walking asking to pay for sex. Punkin knew it was the police and told Star he was a police. Thinking Punkin was wrong, Star got in the car, never to return.

Doing my best I tried to get her out. Waiting six hours at Bad Boys Bail Bonds just to find out that she had a Probation hold out of San Francisco also for solicitation. It was a sad ride back to Vallejo that night. All the girls fell asleep on the ride back but Liesha. That night I told her about my trip coming up to Miami. She let me know she had never been out of California and was going to do everything she could to join me.

In two days, Liesha not only got herself a round-trip ticket to Miami, but on the same plane. With me already having the room and everything else covered, she was all smiles. One thing I was sure of was Punkin wouldn't be once she got wind of Liesha joining us. Wasn't no way I was telling Punkin this news. At least not yet, if I could help it.

CHAPTER 30

Our plane landed in Miami, Florida at 3:45pm California time, but with the three hour difference it was now 6:45pm. Making our way to Enterprise rental Car area, where they had there awaiting me an Infinity Truck QX70. Jumping in Punkin, Liesha and I were all ready to live life, the Miami way. The vibe with us felt great, so did every inch of the QX70. Designed to reward your sense with luxury, we hit the main streets feeling like stars. It was a very short ride from North Beach to South Beach where we were staying.

Our room had everything from swimming pool to hot tubs. Tennis courts as well as a game room and work out gym, plus massage. From our patio was the most wonderful sight of the beach and its crystal water. The weekend was said to be when the streets and beaches would be packed. With it only being Tuesday, we had lots of time to learn our way around. We drove deep into the city, from the highway to the Coliseum where the Miami Heat played. Everywhere we went I saw some of the sexiest women walking around wearing almost nothing.

Punkin had posted an add on Backpage about her services and in no time she had dates lining up. As she went on her first date, Liesha and I decided to walk on the beach. Taking our shoes and socks off we walked in the fine, white sand that lined the beach. Holding hands we talked about our dreams and goals, to what I had planned to do to her when we got back into our room. I admired her dignity, a quality I couldn't find in the other girls.

Back in the room, I noticed that Punkin hadn't made it back. Leading the way to the room, Liesha and I undressed. Grabbing her hand, I turned her to face me. Kissing her in her mouth gently and naturally, our kissing turned more passionate. Sitting her down in a chair in the room, I stood behind her and began massaging her neck and shoulders. Slowly her head began to fall forward as her hair covered her face as she allowed herself to fully relax and let my hands do the work.

Fully undressed I laid her on the bed, where I used my tongue to play with her clitoris. Softly, I let my tongue do what my hands couldn't, making her body wiggle in pure pleasure. Sensing she wanted me inside of her, I stood and thrusted inside of her from on top, powerfully. Wrapping her legs around me, she gripped my dick with every muscle inside of her, making me feel welcome and wanted. Easing her legs onto my shoulders, I continued to enter her harder and harder. Feeling her walls begin to flutter as she spilled all her juices like she had lost control. The feeling of her nutting all over my love stick only magnified the good feeling I was already having, making me fill up her hole with some juices of my own. Holding me tightly like she never wanted to let me go, we fell asleep naked in the wetness of our own love making.

Awakened by a cool breeze draft coming through the opened patio window, I could hear the sounds of the waves lapping gently at the shore outside. Seeing Punkin back just sitting in the chair with fire in her eyes, I knew she wasn't pleased to see me and Liesha naked, while she was out making the money that she had put on the dresser for me. Like always Punkin came baring gifts. Putting fourteen hundred on the dresser, she showed me on our first night in town she could and would make money for me anywhere I took her. I had a decision to make soon that was either going to make me or brake me. With so much on my mind, I sat poolside alone relaxing, taking in the sunset. Enjoying a tall glass of ice cold lemonade, Miami was the place to be and I hadn't saw nothing yet. The weekend was yet to come.

Friday came and it was like South Beach had changed overnight. The streets were packed, people everywhere. Traffic was bumper to bumper, moving at a snail's pace. It would be this way for the rest of our stay, so we rented motorbikes to miss the traffic.

It was going to be a big night at Club Teaser's where Dwayne Wade, Rick Ross and Trick Daddy was having a party at the best strip club on Se club was packed from wall to wall. Naked women walked freely in hunt for a big payday. Most of the ballers had a V.I.P. section with their girls performing on their stage. Others got lap dances and took V.I.P. rooms, where the strippers tried their best to fulfill your sexual fantasy for a large fee in privacy.

Punkin met a stripper in the club named Honest. In a pair of high heels that strapped around her ankles, with only a red thong on she was the thickest in the building and receiving all the attention and money. She told Punkin how lucrative stripping was and how much safer it was to meet tricks and get their money. With her being in good with the owner, she promised Punkin a job over her weekend stay.

When the clubs let out, the real party was outside. In a city that didn't sleep we all popped an ecstasy and stayed out all night. From boats to bikes would be our weekend, as Punkin showed a little skin shaking her ass and collecting the cash. Honest really liked Punkin and before we left, Liesha and I walked in on them making out.

CHAPTER 31

Self-made, self-paid was where I was at in my life. Punkin was mad at me once we made it back to California and on top of that so was Sherise. I got home and she was livid. She was done with my bullshit. After being away for a week in Miami without her, she knew there was someone else.

Feeling like shit for all the wrong I had done to her. For years her love had been my shield, her strength and courage, my sword. But I found myself torn between my feelings for Liesha and the girls and my true love with Sherise. Shooken up I had to respect the fact that Sherise and I relationship had run its course. For me to really love her I had to let her go, to find someone to love her the way she truly deserved to be.

Back in the Vistas the mood wasn't quite the same. Things had been tense to say the least after the killing of Pistol Pete. Keyona staying back to get the money I would have missed helped out a lot but only for me, because she was acting done with me as well for not taking her. Keeping a hold on Punkin and Keyona started not to be so easy with

Liesha demanding most of my time. Punkin and Keyona was my bread and butter, but I was about to find out that Keyona no longer wanted to be the bread nor butter that Liesha would eat off of again.

The clouds darkened as a full moon could be seen. All day Keyona had been calling me to meet up with her cousin who she said was in desperate need of a pistol. I agreed to meet him.

Liesha and I rode together to make the sale. Pulling up I saw to guys standing outside a car with two females in the back seat. One being Keyona so I was a little more relaxed. The closer I got to the car, the other girl also looked very familiar, but in the dark I couldn't make out where I knew her from. The two guys walked up on my car as I pulled up. Getting out with the gun in my hands, we all walked over to the porch in front of where we were parked. With there not being much lighting on the porch, I suggested we go inside and do the deal.

"Let's just do it right here, because my Auntie be tripping." The shorter of the two replied. He was also the driver of the car. The other guy was more slim and tall, with a baby face. Trying to get to the business we were here for, I opened up the .357 snub nose pistol and took out all the bullets before handing it over to the shorter guy.

Holding the pistol he looked over it, as if he was checking it out, before asking, "Show me again how you opened it up to take the bullets out?"

Taking the gun out of his hands, I reshowed him how to open it. Then gave it to him again. As he began to call himself checking it out again, is when I felt that something wasn't right and grab for my gun back.

"Look here my nigga I ain't with no shit, your cousin is my girl, so if something you find is wrong with it just call me, so either you want it or you don't." I said very seriously ready to get out of there, feeling out of place where I was.

"Okay, okay, it's all good." The shorter one said with attitude in his voice. Seeing I was now growing impatient, he acted as if he was reaching in his pocket to get the cash, but instead reached at his waistline where he had a 40 glock hanging. Looking over at his friend he gave an almost imperceptible nod.

Seeing the handle of his gun I reacted fast and first, rushing him into the wall, making the gun on his hip to fall in the inside of his pants leg. The taller one standing behind me hit me in the back of the head with something that felt like metal. Mind only on not letting the shorter one get to his pistol, I didn't even feel the hit to the head. Once my mind got to working, I put together that it felt like metal I was hit with, I looked back to see the taller one pointing a gun at me.

Releasing the guy I was wrestling with, I yelled out, "Nooooo," as loud as I could as I ran into him like a running back trying to get into the end zone. Hitting him with a hard shoulder, I kept running right passed him. I hit a gate and saw that they were not giving chase, instead was heading to my car where Liesha was. Making her give up her belongings and the keys, the shorter one jumped in my car and burned rubber.

Crying my name out loud I could hear Liesha. Knowing it was safe, I hopped the gate and rushed to her. We walked to my Mom's house where I had another car and called the police to report my car stolen. Sitting in my Mom's house I replayed everything. Keyona had for sure set me up, and it hit me who the girl in the back was. It was Drea. How could I forget her face? It all started making sense, and the guy wasn't Keyona's cousin that was Drea's man, he had gotten out and wanted his money back.

Liesha and I had almost lost our lives. Mama prayed over us and let me know once again God had shown favor in me. Leaving her feeling more thankful than mad, we headed home.

They always said when it rains it pours. Like a domino effect, everything started falling apart. When I got over to the apartment I had for the girls, it was empty. Punkin had took everything and headed for the border. After talking with the neighbors, the news I heard from them was inconceivable. Punkin had ran off with my man Nate. I had beaten her down physically and mentally too many times. Hearing about Liesha pregnancy by me was her last straw.

CHAPTER 32

The robbery situation really was an eye opener and time for a change. Taking my winnings, I decided to move me and Liesha out of Vallejo. I went from having a harem to just having her. On the fourth of July, the police caught Drea's boyfriend driving my S55 Mercedes with her and Keyona all in the car. With it being reported stolen and not high jacked he was only charged with joyriding, GTA and the others were let go.

With God being so good to me, I started to be good to myself as well as my two sons. Being in the house more, bonding with Liesha and our kids, life began to show its meaning, something I was missing out on running the streets. The responsibility of being a father. Liesha 13 weeks with my first daughter, I was already in love with.

Liesha already had a daughter of her own named Ce-Ce. From day one Ce-Ce and I bonded. Looking just like her mother, she was a beautiful little girl. Her and my youngest son Damonte' brought the family together as one. They grew up together and grew to be very close. When my oldest son Little David would come over, being so much older than the two, he was very helpful in helping them out and they respected him a lot. However he also showed signs of missing us being with Sherise and Mar-Mar who was like his brother after all the years I spent with Sherise. But things had changed and this was our new family.

August 6th and Liesha's water busted. I had been a part of taking a life, even sparing a few, but being a part of bringing life into the world, it could be life changing. Watching my seed come out of her womb left me speechless. Bringing me back to reality, the Doctor handed me the scissors to cut the cord.

The nurse took the baby over to a nearby table to clean all the blood off her before wrapping her up real tight and returning her to me. She was mine, she had my eyes, lips, skin tone and my last name. With both my boys' names already starting with the letter "D", I wanted to keep that going naming her Destiny. The delivery went great, Destiny was born with all her toes, fingers, her hearing as well as her eyesight. God was still in the business of blessing me, and I was counting them.

Six weeks of being home, Liesha was ready to get back working. Her job needed her it being the holiday season coming she could make some good money. Her back at work made me the stay-at-home Dad. Damonte', Ce-Ce, Destiny and I spent a lot of time together, turning me from a boy to a man. Seeing that I was the leader, I began teaching them how to spell their names, how to count, read and spell. Anything I could do to better prepare them for life and every moment felt good.

The more I would teach them the more they wanted to learn. Everything I put into my kids came out. My relationship and love for my kids grew to heights I never knew. God was opening doors I didn't even know could open and when Liesha came to me with the idea of us all going to church I embraced it and we were all in.

Church was a place we would go each Sunday to give thanks and praise our God. It also seemed to bring us closer together as a family. The more we went the more into it I got. It was the learning of the Word that was best for me and my kids. Teaching them who they could call on when mama and daddy couldn't be. I knew that lesson alone would one day help them in life.

CHAPTER 33

Four years had passed and Liesha and I were still together. She had upgraded our lives by leaving Walmart and working for the US Postal Service as a mail carrier, making $12 more and benefits for the whole family.

As I stood outside of our new home, as a home owner, I looked up to the sky as the stars made their evening debut. I was thankful for everything I was blessed with up until this point. My life had never been going better. We were on the right track, heading in the right direction.

Something divine and strong came over Liesha's and my relationship. It was more influential than sex. It was beautiful, perfect and extremely dangerous. I was in love with her.

It was Valentine's Day and we were spending it in Reno, Nevada to tie the knot. The limo came to get us from our room. In her strapless, white dress that draped over her shapely frame, Liesha got in first as the driver held open the door for us both, before taking us to the Chapel.

Standing up face to face, Liesha and I exchanged our vows. Pouring out my innermost feelings, I stated every word of my vows. Eyes watering she said hers back. Hair hung in her face and down passed her soft shoulders, she moved it all out the way as I took her into my arms as our mouths met to enjoy the most incredible kiss ever.

Back inside the awaiting limo were two glasses of wine, some balloons and a card. Picking up the card as she poured the wine, I read it out loud to her.

"May this day, you two cherish forever. In the Holy book in Proverbs 18:22, it says, 'Who is findeth a wife, findeth a good thing and obtaineth favor of the Lord.' 1 Corinthians 7:2 also says, 'Nevertheless to avoid fornication let every man have his own wife and every woman have her own husband.' May God be with you both.

Putting the card down we shared another kiss before drinking our cups of wine. Holding hands we went to our room. Inside there was a path of rose petals leading from the door to the bed, another set leading to the hot tub, where more wine awaited us. Lit candles were all through the room. Getting in her sexy but not at all sleazy lingerie, we made love everywhere we could until she passed out. Looking at her naked body as she slept I said a prayer.

"Dear God,
    I thank you for blessing me with a beautiful wife and family. As we set out to raise our family led by you, forgive us for our sins and protect us from harm."

Whispering, "Amen", I kissed my wife turning over to hit the light, when my phone rang. It was Mama so I answered.

"Congratulation Son, I love you dearly and had to call yall and say I love both of yall. I wish yall nothing but the best." She said sincerely.

"Thank you so much Mom and I love you even more." I told her, thankful for having such a supportive mother.

"Son a package also came here for you from U.P.S." she stated.

"What was in it? Did you open it up?" I asked knowing my mother was very nosey.

"I sure did, it was something called an embosser, a reader writer and a new laptop."

TO BE CONTINUED.........

CHAPTER #1

"Truth Be Told"

"Chow Time, Chow Time,". Was the loud voice of the sheriff coming through the intercom in my cell in the Santa Rita Jail, as the sound of doors popping open followed. After 14 years long of freedom I couldn't believe I was back in here again. Picking up the newspaper, I headed back to my cell. I had no appetite for chow. Nevertheless, I couldn't wait to read what the media had to say about me this time in the newspapers. It was on the front page of the East Bay Times.

"Ex-con charged in East Oakland fatal shooting." An ex-convict who survived being shot 12 times in 2005 and was acquitted three years before that for his role in an earlier killing has been charged with murder again, as well as other counts in the fatal shooting May 15 of a man near an East Oakland Elementary School according to authorities.

David A. Buchanan, 39, of Oakland was charged Monday in the killing of a unknown man in the 2200 block of East 17th street near Garfield Elementary school. Besides the murder count Buchanan is also charged with two counts of possession of a firearm by a felon, and two counts of carrying a loaded firearm on ones person in a city. According to court records, Buchanan has three prior felony convictions.

Police believe the two men were acquainted with each other before the fatal shooting, which happened about 3:06 Am May 15. Buchanan was driving a van which was stopped when the shooting happened after the victim approached the vehicle and interaction " took place," the documents say. The victim, was able to make it a short distance away after being shot before collapsing and was later pronounced dead at the scene. According to the police, the shooting was captured on video in the area, which showed Buchanan exiting the van and picking up something before driving away.

Based on the video and other evidence, police were able to identify Buchanan as the suspect, officers said. He was arrested May 16 driving the van in the 2300 black of Foothill Boulevard. A loaded gun was found under the driver seat and another gun was found at his home were police served a search warrant. According to the police documents, Buchanan's prior felony convictions are for transportation for sales of a controlled substance in Alameda County in March 2000 and possession for sale of a controlled substance and possession of a firearm by a felon in January 2017 in Solano county. He received prison sentences for all his convictions. David is now being held in Santa Rita County Jail.

Police also states Buchanan was shot 12 time in August 2005, While he stood in front of a shrine in the 2000 black of 23rd Avenue in East Oakland for a homicide victim. Buchanan Some how survived the shooting, and with him being uncooperative no one has ever been arrested in his shooting.

Buchanan, was also one of two men prosecuted in March 2001 fatal shooting of another man in the 1700 block of 28th Avenue in a drug related dispute. Buchanan accompanied the gunman to the scene and was charged under the state felony Murder rule. Buchanan was acquitted by a 12 person jury in October 2002, the accused gunman was convicted.

Letting the newspaper drop from my hands, it was all surreal in a way I haven't anticipated. With tears in my eyes, I laback down knowing that violence and tragedy had once again entered my life and the media was doing their best to trash my name. Determine, my demeanor changed and I knew my day would soon come for the truth to be told.......

Part 3 Coming Soon....

Lightning Source UK Ltd.
Milton Keynes UK
UKHW022203231219
355907UK00006B/107/P